The Anglo-Norman Voyage of St Brendan
Bilingual edition

J S Mackley

Copyright © 2014 J S Mackley

New Edition 2025 Published by Isengrin Publishing

Published by Isengrin Publishing, Northampton

Set in Garamond

All rights reserved. No part of this publication may be reproduced, stored in any retrieval system, or transmitted, in any form or by any means, electronic, mechanical, photocopying, recording or otherwise except for the purpose of academic study, without the prior permission of the publishers.

ISBN: 978-1-917130-09-7

www.jonmackley.com

For Glyn Burgess

ACKNOWLEDGMENTS

The transcription of this volume is based on the text reconstructed by E.G.R Waters (1890–1930) published as *The Anglo-Norman Voyage of Brendan by Benedeit* (Oxford: Clarendon Press, 1928). The English translation is a revised version of a version previously published as an appendix to J.S. Mackley, *The Legend of Brendan* (Leiden: Brill, 2008). The revisions have drawn on Glyn Burgess's translation in *The Voyage of St Brendan: Representative Versions of the Legend in English Translation*, eds. W.R.J. Barron and Glyn S. Burgess, (Exeter: University of Exeter Press, 2002; 2nd Revised edition 2005): 65–102.

I am grateful to J.W. Mackley who assisted with the translation, as well as Nick Havely, Glyn Burgess and Jonathan Wooding, all of whom were instrumental in the development of this work.

First folio: British Library, Cotton Vespasian B.x
(MS A of the Anglo-Norman *Voyage*)

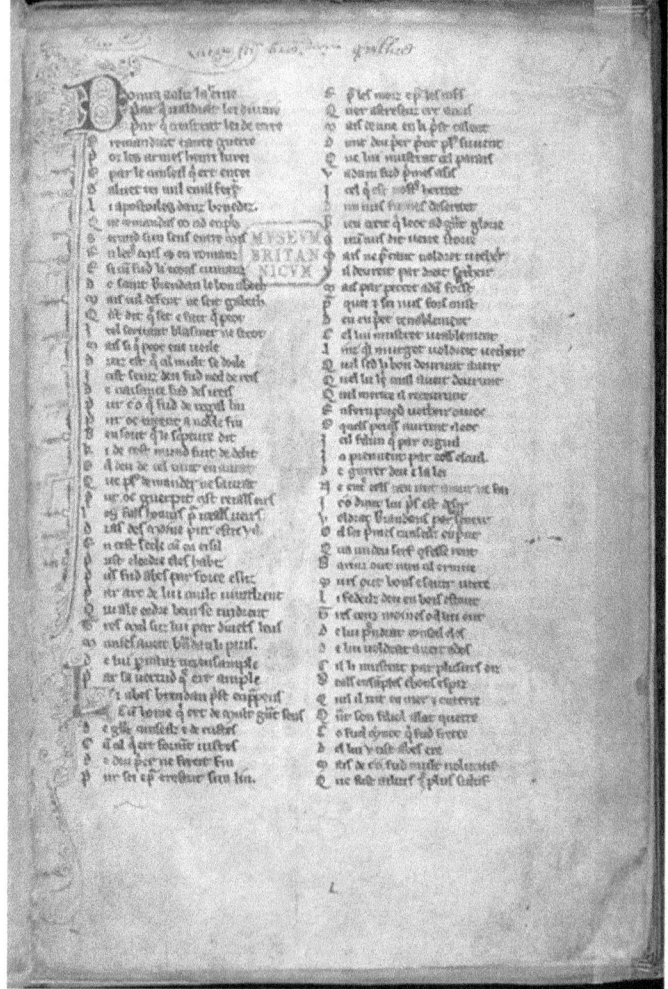

DISCUSSION

The Anglo-Norman Version

E.G.R Waters's reconstruction of the Anglo-Norman *Voyage of Brendan* was published in 1928 by the Clarendon Press. It did not receive a wide circulation in this form as many of the warehoused copies were pulped during the Second World War. Waters's edition is a scholarly work which includes a comparison with its primary source material, the Latin *Nauigatio Sancti Brendani abbatis*, as well as a discussion of versification, the phonology of the author, a classification and *stemma* of the manuscripts and a discussion of the relationship with later Latin prose and rhymed versions.[1]

There are other editions and translations of the Anglo-Norman versions of the Brendan legend:

- Benedeit, *The Anglo Norman* Voyage of St Brendan, Eds. Ian Short and Brian Merrilees (Manchester: Manchester University Press, 1979).
- Glyn S. Burgess, 'The Anglo-Norman Version' in *The Voyage of St Brendan: Representative Versions of the Legend in English Translation*, eds. W.R.J. Barron and Glyn S. Burgess, (Exeter: University of Exeter Press, 2002; 2nd Revised edition 2005): 65–102.

---

[1] E.G.R. Waters, ed., *The Anglo-Norman Voyage of St Brendan by Benedeit* (Oxford: Clarendon Press, 1928); the Latin version is published as Carl Selmer, ed., *Nauigatio Sancti Brendani abbatis from Early Latin Manuscripts*, Publications in Mediaeval Studies, 16 (Notre Dame: University of Notre Dame Press, 1959).

o Ian Short and Brian Merrilees, *Le Voyage de Saint Brendan, éd. bilingue, texte, traduction, présentation et notes* (Paris: Champion Classiques, 2006).

Authorship and patron

The Anglo-Norman *Voyage of Brendan* was written during the reign of Henry I of England (1100–35). The author identifies himself as 'danz Benedeiz' – 'brother Benedeit'.[2] It is assumed that he was a Benedictine monk of Norman extraction, but there has been little plausible evidence as to who he was, we only know that he claims he has taken the poem 'en letre' – in Latin, and translated it into the vernacular 'en romanz'.[3]

The version of the poem presented here is dedicated to Henry's second wife Adeliza of Louvain who came to England and married in 1121. She died in 1151. As a patron of the arts commissioning Phillippe de Thaün's *Bestiary* and a (now lost) *chançon* celebrating the life of her husband, Adeliza is generally accepted as the patroness of the *Brendan* as declared in the first line: 'Donna Aaliz la reïne' and as the poem describes events in the future, it is plausible that it dates from shortly after Adeliza's arrival in England and marriage to Henry in Windsor Castle on 29 January 1121.[4]

The dedication of the poem, however plausible, is challenged by one of the surviving manuscript fragments

---

[2] E. Wahlberg, 'Sur le nom de l'auteur du *Voyage de saint Brendan*,' *Studia Neophilologica* 12 (1939): 46–55, p. 55.

[3] M. Dominica Legge, *Anglo-Norman Literature and its Background* (Oxford: Clarendon Press, 1963), p. 9.

[4] J.R.H. Weaver, ed., *The Chronicle of John of Worcester 1118–1140* (Oxford: Clarendon Press, 1908), pp. 15–16. Cf. Agnes Strickland, *The Lives of the Queens of England* (London: Henry Colburn, 1840), vol. 1, pp. 212–56.

(MS C) which opens with the line: "De mahalt la reine" referring to Maud, or Matilda, of Scotland, Henry's first wife who was the daughter of Malcolm III (Canmore) and St Margaret. As a Scot she may have been more interested in the life of a Celtic saint.

Could the poem have been dedicated to Matilda in 1100 and the rededicated to Adezlia in 1121? This is unlikely. It is probable that this was no more than a later scribe's association with the earlier queen. It is more likely that Adeliza, whose first language was French and who took more interest in her husband's affairs of state, commanded that the original Latin poem was translated for the amusement of her courtiers who did not speak Latin.

Origin of the legend

St Brendan the Navigator (b. *c.* 486, d. 575–583) is the patron saint of boatmen, mariners, travellers, elderly adventurers and whales. His feast day is 16 May.

Born in the sept of Altraige, near Tralee in County Kerry, he was abbot of Clonfert, where he founded the church in 563. Most of the texts that we have about Brendan concern his voyage to the Otherworld, stories which were probably developed in an oral tradition at the beginning of the ninth century.[5]

Historical evidence for Brendan is sketchy. The earliest surviving manuscript evidence was written at least a century after his death: Brendan is mentioned in the *Vita Columbæ* by Adomnán (679–704); in addition, versions of Brendan's

---

[5] Jonathan M. Wooding, 'The Date of the *Nauigatio S. Brendani Abbatis*,' *Studia Hibernica,* vol. 37 (2011): 9–26, pp. 23, 26. Based on Dicuil's writing and the desertion of the Faeroes, Wooding suggests the *Nauigatio* was not composed before 795, and, based on the manuscript evidence, no later than 950.

life in Latin and Irish were circulated only two centuries after his death. Some of these accounts of Brendan's life became conflated with the later stories of his marvellous voyage; however, the earliest forms of his life (known as the *vita altera* in the *Codex Salmanticensis*) were not only particularly corrupted, but they were also 'ruthlessly abbreviated' for the purposes of reading in Church.'[6] These lives of Brendan give details of his birth and baptism in a manner similar to the birth and baptism of Jesus in St Matthew's Gospel: his name derives from the white mist (*broan finn*) that rises when he is born. At the time of his birth St Patrick, patron saint of Ireland, predicts that Brendan will be a great patriarch.[7]

As a child, Brendan is tutored by Bishop Erc; he performs minor miracles and demonstrates his piety which includes the conversion of a great warrior and raising a dead man back to life. His piety is such that angels minister to him and command him to write an ecclesiastical rule. Brendan was ordained by Erc around 501. After this event, the details of Brendan's life become conflated with the story of his voyage to the Promised Land of the Saints.

One version of the *vita* describes Brendan as undertaking two voyages. The first is in a skin-covered coracle; the monks have many encounters during the five-year voyage. However, Brendan fails to find the Promised Land. On his return to Ireland, Brendan's foster-mother, St Ita, explains that he should travel in a wooden boat, rather than

---

[6] Charles Plummer, *Lives of Irish Saints*, 2 vols (Oxford: Clarendon Press, 1922),vol. 1, p. xviii; Richard Sharpe, *Medieval Irish Saints: An Introduction to the Vitae sanctorum Hiberniae* (Oxford: Clarendon Press, 1991), p. 368.

[7] Whitley Stokes, 'Notes on the Life of St Brendan,' *Irish Ecclesiastical Record* 8 (October 1871–February 1872), 17–25, 79–86, 178–190 and 193–208, p. 20.

one made from the hides of dead animals. This voyage, which lasts for another two years, is successful and the brethren reach Paradise. However, in the *Nauigatio sancti Brendani abbatis*, the hide boat does not prevent the monks from reaching Paradise; in fact the text describes the building of the coracle in some detail (*caput* VI).

After his return home, Brendan founds a monastery at Clonfert in 558, and, after travelling to Annaghdown to visit his sister, St Bridget, to make arrangements for his internment, he dies at the threshold of the church. His body is returned to Clonfert where it is buried in a grave facing the front door of the cathedral. The Irish annals record that Brendan died in 575–583AD.

The story of the *Voyage of Brendan*

The *Nauigatio sancti Brendani abbatis* (hereafter, the *Nauigatio*) was composed around the start of the ninth century: the purpose, along with other saints' lives (or *vitæ*), was to have a comprehensive narrative for the saints to be read in church.

In the *Nauigatio*, Brendan is given details about the *Insula deliciosum* ('Isle of Delights') and the *Terra repromissionis sanctorum* ('Promised Land of the Saints') by Barrindus, a travelling monk. Inspired, Brendan decides to seek the *Terra repromissionis sanctorum* for himself.

The narrative of the Anglo-Norman version follows the Latin version relatively closely, although Waters observes that Benedeit was an excellent editor, and that he omits much of the tedious liturgical material found in the original Latin version.[8] Arguably, the author of the *Nauigatio* was drawing on some source material, amongst which were

---

[8] Waters, *The Anglo-Norman Voyage*, pp. ci–cii.

Irish voyage tales and voyages to the Otherworld (respectively known as *immrama* and *echtrae*) and some of the imagery was impossible for Benedeit to decode as he was unfamiliar with the source material.

The Anglo-Norman *Voyage* describes how Brendan, an Irish abbot originally of royal lineage, desires to see Paradise and Hell before he dies. He seeks the advice of a hermit called Barrind who explains how he and his godson travelled to an island from which one could see Paradise. Brendan chooses fourteen companions: together they pray and fast and are visited by an angel who authorises their voyage. As they plan to leave in a coracle, Brendan is approached by three additional monks who plead with him to let them join the voyage; Brendan agrees, but warns them that they will not complete the journey.

Setting sail, the monks begin to learn the practicalities of seamanship and to understand the importance of faith. The winds carry them to an island upon which they discover an uninhabited city which has an abundance of food and drink. Brendan cautions them only to take what they need. During the night Brendan witnesses the devil tempting one of the three late-coming brethren to steal a goblet. Although Brendan cautions the brethren not to remove anything from the city, the monk is revealed to be a thief. Brendan dispels the devil from the monk, who receives absolution before he dies.

Preparing to leave the island, the brethren are approached by a mysterious messenger (who the text also refers to as the Procurator, the Host and the Youth in Paradise) who provides them with food and drink and promises them more provisions in the future. The monks then travel to an island of giant sheep where they celebrate

The Anglo-Norman Voyage of St Brendan

Maundy Thursday. The messenger directs them to another island for Easter Day, although this island starts moving when they light their fires and it transpires that it is actually a giant fish.

The next island to which the brethren travel is filled with beautiful birds. One of these explains they were angels who sided with neither God nor Lucifer in the war in Heaven and as a consequence they were expelled from Heaven but not relegated to Hell. The bird explains that the brethren will travel for seven years, returning to key locations for the major feasts, before finally reaching Paradise.

From the Birds' Island, the monks sail to an island which has an ideal monastic community; here the monks receive their food by a mysterious agency and Brendan is told that their lamps are lit by a divine light. Despite Brendan's desire to stay with this community, they are told that they must leave after Epiphany.

Sheltering from a storm on another island, the monks discover a spring. Brendan warns the brethren to drink in moderation; however the monks drink to excess and are intoxicated. When they awaken they begin their cyclical voyage again, first coming to the Island of Sheep, the Island Fish and the Paradise of Birds. Their vessel is then attacked by a sea serpent, which is, in turn, attacked by another sea serpent. The remains of the first serpent are washed up onto the shore and feeds the brethren for the next three months. Next, the monks are attacked by a griffin, which is in turn attacked by a dragon. Then, as Brendan celebrates the Feast of St Peter and St Paul, the monks can see huge fish beneath them in the clear ocean; initially, they are terrified, but they realise that the sea creatures are participating in the worship.

From here, the brethren enter supernatural realms: first they see a giant crystal pillar in the ocean from which Brendan takes a chalice for worship. They then arrive at the Smithy of Hell where the demon smith hurls fiery rocks at their coracle; the monks also see Hell itself. Here the second of the supernumeraries jumps overboard and is dragged away by demons. They also find Judas Iscariot on a rock who is allowed a short respite from Hell for the good deeds he performed in his lifetime. Brendan secures an additional day of release from Hell, while Judas describes his routine of tortures and the third supernumerary monk mysteriously disappears. Finally, Brendan meets the antithesis of Judas, a saintly hermit named Paul who describes his virtuous life.

At the end of the seven years, the brethren are joined by the messenger who directs them through a fog barrier that surrounds Paradise.

Amid a vivid description of a fertile land, Brendan sees Paradise atop a high mountain, but is told that his human mind is incapable of appreciating the full wonders of Paradise so the brethren return to Ireland.

The development of the *Nauigatio sancti Brendani*

That the *Nauigatio* was originally composed in Ireland is shown by the 'Hibernicisms' in the text and the author's attention to topographical and genealogical details. He had a strong command of Latin, theology and history, and it is likely he belonged to a monastery. He was also familiar with texts such as *The Marvels of the East* and Biblical Apocrypha. The story of Brendan's travels was immensely popular: it survives in nearly 130 manuscripts dating from the 10th to the 17th century. Some of the content was considered

The Anglo-Norman Voyage of St Brendan

heretical and it is cited in some Inquisition depositions.[9] It has been translated many times including Old Norse, Venetian and Catalan; Similarly, the story was re-worked but contained many familiar themes when it was circulated in Middle German and Middle Dutch. St Brendan's Isle appeared on many medieval maps, including one used by Christopher Columbus. It is sometimes thought to be the eighth of the Canary Islands and apparently inspired many Portuguese and Spanish sailors to search for it.[10]

The *Nauigatio* was primarily composed for the benefit of the brethren in a monastery who considered Brendan as their spiritual guardian. The exciting stories of the ocean would also attract pilgrims (and their generous donations) who were interested in the cult of St Brendan; however, such stories usually contained examples of miracles and healing. Such stories are found in the earlier *vitæ* of Brendan, where Brendan performs miracles, deeds and conversions that are in keeping with a Christian saint, but they are not in the *Nauigatio* itself, where, although miraculous events occur around Brendan, he does not perform them himself. Thirdly, a wider community grew around the monastery: these lay people may have been involved in the farming of the lands, or may have provided skills, and the *Nauigatio*, amongst other texts, would have been read to them for their spiritual edification. However, the earliest manuscripts describing the *Nauigatio* begin

---

[9] Peter Biller, Caterina Bruschi and Shelagh Sneddon (eds.), *Inquisitors and Heretics in Thirteenth-Century Languedoc: Edition and Translation of Toulouse Inquisition Depositions, 1273–1282* (Leiden: Brill, 2010), pp. 578–89.

[10] Clara Strijbosch, 'Searching for a Versatile Saint' in *The Brendan Legend: Texts and Versions*, ed. G.S. Burgess and Clara Strijbosch (Leiden: Brill, 2006), p. 1.

incipit vita Sancti which indicates that the scribes believed that what they were copying was a saint's life or hagiography.

Is it possible that Brendan's voyage represents an actual journey? In 1976, Tim Severin proved that it is possible to travel from Ireland to America in a coracle similar to the one described in the *Nauigatio*.[11] The *Landnámabók* – the Icelandic Book of Settlements – mentions Irish monks settling in Iceland before 795, although Sigrid Kaland argues that these books were based on the oral tradition and were written some three centuries after the events they describe.[12] It is tempting to see parallels between the descriptions in the text and geographical locations: the name of the Faeroes in Old Norse is *Færeyjar*, literally, 'the island of sheep' and the Islands have a sheep on their coat of arms. Furthermore, it was customary for medieval navigators to leave sheep on an island in anticipation of future voyages. Dicuil, a geographer writing in 825, describes the Faeroe islands as a haven for anchorites;[13] the coagulated sea could be seen to be the northern ice pack; the crystal column could be a glacial ice shelf; the demon smithy could be an Icelandic volcano; and Judas may receive his respite from Hell on Rockall. The journey may end in Newfoundland.[14] All of these are plausible explanations; but rather than one person making

---

[11] Timothy Severin, *The Brendan Voyage* (London: Abacus, 1996).

[12] J.J. Tierney, (ed.), *Dicuili Liber de mensura orbis terrae* (Dublin: Dublin Institute for Advanced Studies, 1967), VII, 11, p. 75, 115; Ari Thorgilsson, *Landnámabók*, trans. Thomas Ellwood (Kendal: T. Wilson, 1898); Sigrid Kaland, 'Comments on 'The Early Settlement of Iceland',' *Norwegian Archaeological Review* 24 (1991), 10–12, p. 10.

[13] Tierney, *Dicuili Liber de mensura orbis terrae*, VII, 15, p. 77.

[14] Other scholars who suggest that the encounters on Brendan's voyage are based on actual locations include George A Little, *Brendan the Navigator* (Dublin, M.H. Gill and Son Ltd, 1945) and Geoffrey Ashe, *Land to the West* (London: Collins, 1962).

the journey himself, the *Nauigatio* is more likely to be a collection of travellers' tales that have gathered around Brendan to act as a backdrop against which he becomes the figurehead to illustrate the faithful, pious life. However, by focusing on the geography, scholars are distracted from the message of the *Nauigatio* and the study of the sources that the narrative uses. The *Nauigatio* uses Biblical, Classical and Apocryphal exemplar to shroud natural exotica in mystery to convey a Christian message of salvation.

Sources for the *Nauigatio*: The Irish *Immrama*

The *Nauigatio* builds on an important Irish tradition of voyaging, but it also drew on classical motifs. In the monastic context, Irish anchorites sailed to islands of the Atlantic to find solitude. These eremitic elements are particularly illustrated in the *Nauigatio* when Brendan encounters a monastic community who were taught by St Ailbe and the solitary hermit, Paul.

This tradition, along with a strong imagination, gave rise to two types of voyage tales: *echtrae* were concerned with a voyage to the Otherworld; *immrama*, which literally translates as 'rowing about', concerned penitential voyages or exile, whether voluntary or enforced.[15]

The earliest of the *immram* tradition influencing the Brendan story is that of *Immram Brain maic Febuil* (*The Voyage of Bran, Son of Febal*), although it is debated as to whether it should be categorised as belonging to the *echtra* or *immram* genre. Séamus Mac Mathúna describes it as a

---

[15] David M. Dumville, '*Echtrae* and *Immram*: Some Problems of Definition,' *Ériu* 27 (1976), 73–94; Mary E. Byrne, 'On the Punishment of Sending Adrift,' *Ériu* 11 (1932), 97–102, p. 97.

'hybrid' containing elements of both genres.[16] The theme of *Immram Brain* is distinctly pagan, whereas the other *immrama* have a distinctly Christian message.

In the later *immrama*, the principal focus is on the voyage itself. In *Immram Snédgusa ocus Maic Riagla* (*Voyage of Snedgus and Mac Riagla*) sixty couples are set adrift for regicide. The clerics, Snedgus and Mac Riagla, accompany them as witnesses. This underscores the difference between imposed punishment and voluntary exile.[17] For those who experience imposed punishment, transgressors were cast into the sea in flimsy vessels with their chances of survival severely reduced. For those who undergo voluntary exile, it could be seen as an act of desperation. (The *Anglo-Saxon Chronicle* entry for 891 records how three Irishmen exiled themselves and reached the court of King Alfred). Sometimes the voluntary exile is an act of piety, just as Christ voluntarily 'exiled' himself from Heaven.

The journey may be penitential: in *Immram curaig Ua Corra* (*Voyage of Húi Corra*), the three leaders of a group of bandits receive a vision and are told to rebuild the churches they destroyed in their raids.[18] Conversely, in *Immram curaig Máele Dúin* (*The Voyage of Máel Dúin's boat*), the protagonist seeks his father's murderers, but because he took on additional passengers, he is blown off course and, during his encounters, he is given time to contemplate his actions

---

[16] Kuno Meyer, (ed). *The Voyage of Bran, Son of Febal, to the Land of the Living: an Old Irish Saga*, 2 vols. (London: D. Nutt, 1895–1897); Séamus Mac Mathúna, *Immram Brain: Bran's Journey to the Land of the Women* (Tübingen: M. Niemeyer, 1985), p. 279.

[17] Whitley Stokes, 'The Voyage of Snedgus and Mac Riagla,' *Revue celtique* 9 (1888): 14–25; see also Byrne, 'The Punishment of Sending Adrift,' p. 101.

[18] Whitley Stokes, 'The Voyage of the Húi Corra,' *Revue celtique* 14 (1893): 22–69.

and ultimately to forgive the murderers.[19]

Although the *Immram* have a Christian message, these stories may have been worked over by Christian scribes after their composition. They still have traces of their pagan heritage. Parts of this can still be seen in the *Nauigatio*. For example the encounter on the Island of Three Choirs in the *Nauigatio* equates to the Island of Laughter in *Immram curaig Máele Dúin*. A crew member is left on each, although for Brendan's monk, it is a blessing, whereas Máel Dúin's foster brother begins his incessant laughter as soon as he touches the island and this him indistinguishable from the other inhabitants.

There are many scenes in the *Nauigatio* that suggest an interborrowing with *Immram curaig Máele Dúin* (for example, the supernumeraries, the deserted citadel, the Island of Laughter and Wailing and the crystal pillar). It appears that a proto-*Máele Dúin* influenced a proto-*Nauigatio* and vice versa; however, the monastic audiences demanded a Christian hero and while Brendan retains the piety shown in the *Vita Brendani*, he does not perform miracles. Instead, while his devotion leads him through the adventures of the *Nauigatio*, the pagan roots have been Christianised.

Hagiography and Romance

The *Nauigatio* prompts us to read it as a hagiography, that is, literature that deals with the lives of Christian saints and

---

[19] Whitley Stokes, 'The Voyage of Máel Dúin,' *Revue celtique* 9 (1888): 447–95; 'The Voyage of Máel Dúin (suite),' *Revue celtique* 10 (1889): 50–95; cf. Elva Johnston, 'A Sailor on the Seas of Faith: The Individual and the Church in *The Voyage of Máel Dúin*,' *European Encounters: Essays in Memory of Albert Lovett*, eds Judith Devlin and Howard B. Clarke (Dublin: University College Dublin Press, 2003), pp. 239–52.

martyrs, but which is 'of a religious character and aims[s] at edification'.[20] The Anglo-Norman *Voyage* is closer to romance. Romance tales are traditionally stories of chivalry and love, or contain matters concerning Rome, Troy, France or England. However, other romance elements included in the Anglo-Norman *Voyage* might include the quest for Paradise as well as striving for spiritual perfection.[21]

Diana Childress identifies the narrative that fits between the two genres of hagiography and romance as 'secular hagiography'.[22] In this type of narrative, the hero may need to call on divine aid to succeed in his quest, thus the text serves to glorify God, rather than to enhance the hero's reputation. Even so, Romance tales are also concerned with the essential qualities of human nature, as well as providing examples of adventure and instruction.[23] Robin Jones argues that the *Voyage* is the first surviving example of Romance in Old French drawing on the previous models of *chansons de geste*.[24] While the *Voyage* was composed well before the recognised beginning of Romance, the genre had been developing over some time before, but these earliest examples would have been oral performances and have since been lost.

Although one might view Brendan's journey as a quest,

---

[20] Hippolye Delehaye, *The Legends of the Saints*, trans. Donald Attwater (London: Geoffrey Chapman, 1962), p. 89.
[21] W.R.J Barron, *English Medieval Romance* (London: Longman, 1987).
[22] Diana T. Childress, 'Between Romance and Legend: "Secular Hagiography" in Middle English Literature,' *Philological Quarterly* 57 (1978), 311–22.
[23] Northrop Frye, *Anatomy of Criticism* (Princeton and Oxford: Princeton University Press, 1971), pp. 33–34.
[24] Robin F. Jones, 'The Precocity of Anglo-Norman and the *Voyage of Saint Brendan*,' *The Nature of Medieval Narrative*, eds Minnette Grunmann-Gaudet and Robin F. Jones, *French Forum Monographs* vol. 22 (Lexington, Kentucky: French Forum Publishers, 1980) 145–58, p. 147.

The Anglo-Norman Voyage of St Brendan

the fact that he returns to Ireland underscores that this should be seen in terms of a pilgrimage. That said, Jonathan Wooding observes that the monks 'are following their monastic vocation with permission and guidance, and alternately fast, pray and row'.[25] Thus, throughout the *Nauigatio*, the emphasis is on the Christian calendar and the monastic day. As well as the lists of psalms and allusions, there are often Biblical allusions and imagery, which underscores the hagiographic nature of the texts.

The message of the *Nauigatio* is one of salvation, although certain early critics found this excessively liberal, most particular considering the treatment of the 'neutral angels' and Judas Iscariot. This message and the concept of the Promised Land of the Saints being reached by a sea voyage were seen by some as heretical and the work was condemned.[26] However, Brendan cannot reach this Promised Land without the piety, obedience and sacrifice required by Christian doctrine.

Source for the Anglo-Norman *Voyage*

When Benedeit composed the Anglo-Norman *Voyage*, he used the *Nauigatio* as his source material. However, he was writing for a different audience and consequently treated the material in a different way. Where the *Nauigatio* was developed from a hagiography and described the deeds of a saint in relation to the monastic calendar, the Anglo-Norman version was composed for entertainment (most

---

[25] Jonathan M. Wooding, 'Introduction' in *The Voyage of St Brendan: Representative Versions of the Legend in English Translation*, ed. W.R.J. Barron and Glyn S. Burgess, 2nd ed. (Exeter: University of Exeter Press, 2005), p. 24.
[26] Paul Meyer, 'Satire en vers rythmiques sur la légende de saint Brendan,' *Romania* 31 (1902), 376–79.

likely for Queen Adeliza's courtiers); consequently Benedeit placed more emphasis on the adventure, which brought the narrative closer to the romance genre. In addition, while there are maxims throughout the Anglo-Norman version, the emphasis is significantly less ecclesiastical than the *Nauigatio*, which contains long lists of psalms and descriptions of the monastic hours. Furthermore, the author of *Nauigatio* included Irish literature and details of Irish genealogies, topography and skills among his source material, but this would not be of interest to Benedeit's audience and was also omitted.

Manuscript evidence

Therr are six surviving manuscripts of the Anglo-Norman *Voyage*, two of which are fragments. The earliest of these dates from the around 1200. Of these manuscripts, three of them begin *Incipit vita Sancti Brendani* and there are Christian maxims throughout. Rather than being written in prose, like the *Nauigatio*, the *Voyage* is written in octosyllabic couplets. Likewise, although the *Voyage* follows the structure of the *Nauigatio*, the focus of the narrative is on the encounters, rather than on their religious message. This is most clearly seen in the Deserted Citadel, for example, where there are descriptions of wealth; or in the extended treatment of Judas Iscariot, which includes graphic descriptions of the two hells and Judas's daily tortures therein.

Key Scenes

There are some principal scenes in the Anglo-Norman *Voyage* that are most memorable. These events also appear in the re-workings of the narrative such as the Middle

The Anglo-Norman Voyage of St Brendan

Dutch and the Middle German versions. These scenes are: the arrival of the supernumeraries; the role of the messenger; and the locations where the brethren celebrate the principal festivals of the monastic year (Jasconius, the island fish; the Paradise of Birds and the Island of the Community of Ailbe). Then there are other scenes that mark Brendan's travels into the Otherworld (the Crystal Pillar and the Smithy of Hell) prior to Brendan's last encounters: with Judas Iscariot; Paul the Hermit; and finally the descriptions of Paradise.

The Supernumeraries

In both versions, after Brendan has chosen his companions, three late-coming monks arrive and threaten to drown themselves if they are not allowed to travel with Brendan. In the *Nauigatio*, the supernumeraries leave in three scenes: The Deserted Citadel, the Island of the Three Choirs and the Smoke-Capped Mountain.

The motif of the late-coming brothers is also seen in *Immram curaig Máele Dúin* when Máel Dúin's foster brothers demand to join the crew; Máel Dúin had been told that additional crew members would upset the balance, and it is because of them that the boat is blown off course, but Máel Dúin is given time to forgive his father's murderers.

Each scene involving the supernumeraries in the *Nauigatio* has a corresponding scene in *Immram curaig Máele Dúin*. First there is a deserted citadel where a cat is found playing among the pillars; however, when one of the foster brothers steals a necklet, the cat changes into a flaming arrow which kills the crew member. Furthermore, the Island of the Three Choirs and the Smoke-Capped mountain both have allusions to *Immram curaig Máele Dúin*: in each encounter one of the foster brothers lands on the island, and immediately that he does so, he begins either laughing or wailing and becomes indistinguishable from the other inhabitants.

In both the *Nauigatio* and the Anglo-Norman *Voyage*, Brendan predicts that one of the three late-coming monks will reach Paradise. The first supernumerary leaves when the monks arrive at a Deserted Citadel. Brendan cautions the monks not to take anything without permission. Despite this warning, Brendan witnesses the Devil entering one of the monks, inspiring him to conceal an object – in the *Nauigatio* it is a silver bridle, in the Anglo-Norman *Voyage* it is a golden goblet. When Brendan challenges the thief, the devil bursts from his chest. The monk repents and achieves Salvation before he dies immediately afterwards.

In the *Nauigatio*, the second monk leaves the crew in an encounter that is omitted from the Anglo-Norman *Voyage*. In the *Nauigatio*, Brendan discovers three choirs: boys, adults and seniors who incessantly move around the island singing psalms. Brendan tells one of the supernumeraries that he may stay as a reward. The author of the Anglo-Norman *Voyage* omitted this scene, primarily because Benedeit's version avoids the overly ecclesiastical tone of its Latin predecessor. Furthermore, this scene is an example of how Benedeit is uncomfortable with the Irish imagery and thus omits it. However, as the author of the *Nauigatio* associated the Island of Laughter with a place of happiness, Brendan was willing to leave the supernumerary there. Thus, with the fate of the supernumerary unresolved, Benedeit had to create a short additional scene after Judas is dragged back to Hell by the devils. At this point the brethren count their number and realise that one is missing – they do not know what has become of him ('E ne sevent qu'est devenuz' l. 1501); however, Brendan tells them that 'God has done with him what pleased Him ... judgement, has been passed on him, either for rest or for torment' which suggests that he *does* know the monk's fate. In addition, as the supernumerary disappeared after the devils take Judas away, the inference is that he was also taken by them.

The other supernumerary that leaves the crew (the third in the *Nauigatio*, the second in the Anglo-Norman *Voyage*) does so after the crew encounter the Demon Smithy and approach the Smoke-Capped Mountain. Here, for an unexplained reason, one of the monks leaps overboard on account of his sins. Although the monks do not see what becomes of their compatriot, Brendan witnesses him being dragged to his damnation by devils.

Thus, in the *Nauigatio*, the fates of the supernumeraries represent the three states of the soul after death: achieving Paradise through good deeds; achieving Paradise through repentance; and damnation. In the Anglo-Norman *Voyage*, however, the message of the supernumeries is ambivalent: once again we see the possibility of achieving salvation through repentance, and the damnation of one of the monks. The fate of the third monk is unknown, and one may speculate that he may be subjected to a series of purgatorial punishments, but will ultimately achieve salvation. However, when the supernumeraries first arrive, Brendan cautions that one of them would be tempted but protected by God – presumably the monk that died in the Uninhabited City. The other two would be taken by Satan, just as he had taken Abiram and Dathan (Numbers 16:33).

These two rebels were swallowed by the ground, along with others who revolted against Moses: this suggests that a hellish fate awaits the last two supernumeraries.

The inclusion of the supernumeraries warns the respective audiences that, despite the divine sanction, the outcome of the journey is uncertain and that not all of the brethren will survive the voyage. It is only once the supernumeraries have left the crew that the remaining brethren can complete their pilgrimage.

The Messenger

The first appearance of a divine guide in the Anglo-Norman *Voyage* is as the monks leave the apparently deserted city. Here he is referred to as a messenger (l. 356). Although the messenger provides food and water, his principal function is to encourage the brethren. Through the fate of the supernumerary, the monks have seen that any transgression is dealt with swiftly and severely. Yet he tells them that God will grant them good fortune and they should have no concern about a lack of provisions in the future (l. 326ff). The monks are not given an opportunity to question him, however. He leaves without another word (l. 370).

The first messenger is not the brethren's regular helper: his first appearance comes in the next encounter and one might be forgiven for initially thinking that the messengers might act as a narrator through each of the scenes. However, this is not the case: Benedeit clearly distinguishes between this messenger – the host – and the one that previously appeared: the host has snow-white hair and youthful eyes. The narrative explains that he brings them unleavened bread 'from his own country', suggesting that he is not from this island. The previous messenger has no description at all. This is substantiated by the fact that the former is referred to as 'un message', while the latter is initially referred to as 'uns mes' (l. 405), although his white hair is described. In both cases, then, the messengers are referred to with an indefinite article. Afterwards the host – the youthful-eyed messenger – is referred to in familiar terms: 'le Deu fedeil' – God's faithful servant (l. 582); 'Lur hoste, le veil chanud' – their host, the white haired old man (l. 827). In the final scene, a youth (who is neither of these messengers, but a resident of Paradise) is referred to as 'un juvencel' (l. 1721). It is tempting to consider that these characters – the Youth and the host – are the same, however, lines 1811–16 show that there are two people: 'Li juvenceals' and 'lur hostes'.

Although the principal aid on this journey is described as a messenger, he is not forthcoming about the island. Benedeit himself interrupts the narrative stating 'I do not know how helpful he was' ('ne sai s'osat,' l. 414) and further that he said 'a little about it' ('mais poi l'en dist,' l. 414).[27] Instead the host serves to dismiss any suggestion of the supernatural – the brethren initially meet him on an island when they are overawed by the sheep which are as large as stags, although the host is adamant that this is not a marvel – *n'est merveille* – and he provides a rational explanation that the large size of the creatures is because the sheep are never milked and because of the clement climate (ll. 420–1).

The youthful-eyed messenger appears secretive; however, there is another level to his communication: that

---

[27] This translation is by Glyn Burgess, although it is a problematic line and other translators, such as Ian Short, disagree.

of *mis*-information. He has the semblance of a guide and directs the monks towards their next location, but he tells them that they will be landing on an island 'en cel' isle anuit estras' (l. 425). This is a practical joke: the 'island' is not an island at all, but a giant fish called Jasconius who takes exception to the monks lighting a fire on his back. Thus, Jasconius is set up to be a surprise. The host describes it as an island that the monks must visit, although he sardonically adds that they will not stay there long.

When the brethren next meet the host, they celebrate the Last Supper together and he performs the ceremony of the washing of the brethren's feet. Thus, the voice of authority willingly becomes the slave of the brethren: the Gospel of John, which describes Jesus' washing of the disciples' feet, describes how 'no messenger is greater than the one who sent him' (John 13:16). The significance then is that Brendan meets a variety of people on his journey, each of whom has a greater understanding of the divine than Brendan himself, but they are still servants of God. In neither the *Nauigatio* nor the Anglo-Norman *Voyage* does Brendan encounter human beings who need to be converted to Christianity: his role is as a navigator and spiritual guide, rather than a converter, and the messenger and the host are agents to help him on his way.

When we consider the provision of food and information – and that is indeed the primary function of both the messenger and the host – then it is worth considering the characters in the context of two scenes in which they do not appear: the first is within a seemingly deserted citadel where the brethren find an abundant supply of food and drink. We know that the host was there, as he appears shortly after the death of one of the brethren. Thus, on this occasion, the presence of the messenger could negate any sense of the miraculous with regard to the provision of food.

The second unexplained provision of food is in the perfect community of the monks of Ailbe where loaves for each of the resident brethren arrive each morning, with an extra supply in anticipation of Brendan's visit. No one sees how this food arrives although the abbot explains that he finds it 'ready each day without having to ask for it' (l. 747–8). The miraculous provision of food is a common hagiographic theme appearing in such legends as the *Life of St Anthony*, where, as with the *Voyage of Brendan*, Anthony receives a double portion when receiving a visitor. But it is curious that the resident monks make no effort to find the source of the food. Instead they rely on faith alone and do not allow anything to distract them from their office.

By the end of the seven year journey, although the brethren have learned all of God's mysteries of the ocean, it is still not enough for them to be able to achieve the Promised Land of the Saints: the host must travel with them to act as their guide, indeed he also takes care of the practicalities of the final stages of their journey – 'Cil aprestet tuz lur busuinz' (l. 1635).

This paradisical land to which the host guides them is described as the land over which Adam had dominion: 'le paraïs/ Dunt Adam fud poëstest' (1651–2). It is surrounded by a thick fog, which no one can penetrate without divine assistance: 'Si de Deu n'at la veüe/ Qui poust passer cele nue' (ll. 1657–8). Although the detail is omitted from the Anglo-Norman version, the cloud obscuring Paradise is an echo of the host's own island in the *Nauigatio* which is described as an 'island like a cloud' – *quasi nubes* (*caput* xv, l. 1), suggesting a link between the host and the Divine. In the Anglo-Norman *Voyage*, as the brethren approach the fog (*calin*) it separates into a passage as wide as a street along which the brethren must travel for three days. Conversely, in the *Nauigatio*, a fog envelops the monks' coracle and it is only after a disorientating hour that the monks find themselves on the shores of Paradise.

The description of Paradise in the Anglo-Norman *Voyage* is a mixture of the description of the New Jerusalem in Revelation 21 and the Garden of Eden in Genesis, particularly once the latter has been closed to humanity. There are palaces of brilliant gems, surrounded by a towering wall, guarded by dragons and in front of which whirls a flaming sword. Curiously, the host seems to have no part in the exploration of Paradise – indeed the last mention of him in the Anglo-Norman version was as the vessel travelled through the avenue of cloud. Instead it is a handsome young man (ll. 1721–2) who calms the dragons and summons an angel to still the sword to allow the brethren to enter 'into true glory' (l. 1734).[28]

The youth guides the brethren through Paradise, but never any further than the limits of their human comprehension. The youth declares 'Ne vus leist pas aler avant,/ Quar poi estes a ço savant' ('You are not permitted to go further,/ For you possess too little knowledge for this' ll. 1793–4). They will learn more when their physical bodies do not encumber them. However, as the brethren leave, it appears that the host has been with them all along, and he remains in Paradise as it is his rightful place: 'Quar

---

[28] In Glyn Burgess's translation, the youth and the host are the same person.

paraïs fud sis dreiz fius' (l. 1816).

The mysterious messenger, whether host, messenger, procurator or youth, serves to foreshadow the coming events and thus to fill each audience with a sense of anticipation. Within the context of the narrative, the host is a character who has the ability to predict, or perhaps even predestine, the locations to which the monks will travel at the principal liturgical festivals during the year. He has an abundant supply of food, and provides comfort and information – when he so chooses.

If we consider the host in relation to monastic society, the procurator – which is how the *Nauigatio* refers to the character – was in charge of the monastic estate management and answerable to the prior. In the same way, the host is God's messenger and steward and answerable to God. Thus, the host's role becomes one of management, to ensure that the monks are adequately provided for during the course of their journey. However, this is only to the extent that the brethren must demonstrate the necessary obedience and determination to succeed and that they must perform certain ceremonies in certain places. The host becomes the representation of God while the monks are away from their community: he does not relate to that community in Ireland. He does not appear at the places where the brethren must learn intrinsic lessons by themselves, such as the punishments of Hell and the rewards of faith as described respectively by Judas Iscariot and Paul the Hermit. Nor does he appear when there is food readily available, for example after the conflict of monsters. The host only appears when it is necessary, otherwise he leaves the monks to fend for themselves in the ocean wilderness: too much help would make the pilgrimage seem easy.

It is tempting to think of the host as a representation of Jesus: the guide and provider on our own pilgrimage of Christian life. Patricia Rumsey identifies him as the 'servant' and the 'shepherd', 'the way' (or guide), and 'the Light' in his identification with the *terra repromissionis sanctorum*.[29] It would also be tempting to think of the host as a representation of St Michael – guiding souls to heaven, and with this in mind, perhaps also represented by the Angel who sanctions Brendan's voyage at the beginning of the narrative – and the youth as St Peter who holds the keys to the gates of Heaven. A more likely theory is that they are representations of the prophets Enoch and Elijah, although in a diluted form, as the Anglo-Norman *Voyage* explicitly states that both the host and the Youth belong in the Promised Land of the Saints. These two characters understand God's mysteries, and, like Enoch and Elijah, they wait in Paradise would be those waiting for the end of time.

The Monastic Year

Brendan's voyage lasts for seven years. During this time he travels to principal locations in order to celebrate the major Christian festivals: from Maundy Thursday to Holy Saturday they rest on the Island of Giant Sheep; they spend Easter on the back of Jasconius; they spend two months from the Octave of Pentecost (the Sunday after Whitsun) which was one of the specially privileged octaves during which no other feast could be celebrated; and finally, from Christmas to the Octave of Epiphany, they stay with the Monastic Community of Ailbe. They return to these

---

[29] Patricia M. Rumsey, *Sacred Time in Early Christian Ireland* (London: T & T Clark Ltd, Continuum, 2007), pp. 182–88.

The Anglo-Norman Voyage of St Brendan

locations each year. Only once the brethren have completed their seven-year cyclical voyage can the monks move towards their final encounters and the knowledge they need that will lead them towards Paradise.

Easter – The Island of Sheep and Jasconius

The brethren spend Maundy Thursday on an island that has sheep 'as large as stags' which they prepare for the sacrifice on Easter Day. The brethren also meet the messenger and when asked why the sheep are so large, he tells them 'it is no marvel: the sheep here are never milked; the weather is not inclement' (ll. 419–422). The messenger then directs them to an island ('Jasconius') where they will celebrate Easter.

The episode with Jasconius is one that is particularly prominent in the various versions of the Brendan legend. In this episode, when the they light a fire to cook a meal, the 'island' moves and is revealed to be a large fish. In the *Nauigatio*, the 'island fish' is given the name 'Jasconius' as a proper noun ('qui habet nomen Jasconius', *caput* x). This name relates to the Irish word *íasc*, meaning fish, and is referred to as *piscis* (fish) or *beluam* (monster), never as a 'whale' (*cetis*, *ballena*).[30]

A similar scene is found in the Sindbad stories and was likely transmitted in a version of the 'Marvels of the East'.[31] Séamus Mac Mathúna argues that the *Physiologus* – a volume of descriptions of animals with a corresponding didactic

---

[30] See Jacqueline Borsje, *From Chaos to Enemy: Encounters with Monsters in Early Irish Texts. An Investigation Related to the Process of Christianization and the Concept of Evil*, Instrumenta Patristica, 29 (Steenbrugge: St-Pieters abdij; Turnhout: Brepols, 1996), p. 35.

[31] Andy Orchard, *Pride and Prodigies: Studies in the Monsters of the Beowulf-Manuscript* (Toronto: University of Toronto Press, 1995), pp. 184–203.

message – is the most likely source for the 'moving island' episode in the *Nauigatio*.[32] Another potential source is the Anglo-Saxon poem 'The Whale' which is included in the Exeter Book.[33] Here, the descriptions of the whale equate to the 'way of devils'. The island upon which the travellers land appears to be a safe haven; the poem and the *Bestiary* equate this to lulling the travellers into a false sense of security before dragging them underwater; or the devil dragging souls to Hell.

In the Brendan legend, however, the first encounter serves to shake the monks from their complacency – the monks spend each Easter in the subsequent years on the back of Jasconius who is shown to be God's servant and helps them understand some of the lessons of faith. When the monks land on the island, they all disembark except for Brendan who stays on board. Once the fire is lit beneath their cauldron and the 'island' begins moving, Brendan tells them not to panic, but instead to put their faith in God.[34] He is in a position to throw ropes and pieces of wood to save them. When the brethren encounter the fish the following year, they find their cauldron still on its back, which helps reassure them (l. 841).

Pentecost – The Neutral Angels

One of the most popular, or perhaps notorious, episodes in Brendan's voyages is that of the Neutral Angels. These are

---

[32] Séamus Mac Mathúna, 'Contributions to a Study of the Voyages of St Brendan and St Malo,' *The Otherworld Voyage in Early Irish Literature*, ed. Jonathan M. Wooding (Dublin: Four Courts Press, 2000), 157–74, p. 171.

[33] Bernard J. Muir, *The Exeter Anthology of Old English Poetry*, 2 vols. (Exeter: University of Exeter Press, 1994), I, pp. 272–75.

[34] Glyn S. Burgess, '*Savoir* and *faire* in the Anglo-Norman *Voyage of St Brendan*,' *French Studies* 49 (1995), 257–74, p. 257.

the angels that sided with neither God nor Lucifer during the War in Heaven (Revelation 12:7–9). As a consequence because they had not sided with God, they were expelled from Heaven; however, because their only crime was apathy, rather than siding with Lucifer, they were not relegated to Hell. Instead, they were granted a place in this terrestrial Paradise of Birds. The geographer Dicuil mentions the island of Vagar, one of the Faeroes, which is famous for its variety of birds and the description of this may correspond with the Paradise of Birds.

The story of the Neutral Angels is not canonical and it is possible that this story developed from two passages from the Book of Revelation. Revelation 12:4 describes how the dragon (who is synonymous with Satan) flicks his tail which 'drew the third part of the stars of heaven and cast them to earth'. This imagery is mixed with Revelation 12:7–9: "there was war in heaven: Michael and his angels fought against the dragon; and the dragon fought and his angels, and prevailed not: neither was their place found any more in heaven. And the great dragon was cast out, that old serpent called the Devil or Satan, which deceiveth the whole world: he cast out into the earth, and his angels were cast out with him.'

This story may also have its roots in the legend of the Watcher Angels or Nephilim: angels who, desiring human women, came down and mated with them (1 Enoch 7–8). They also taught the men forbidden crafts such as witchcraft, sorcery and sword-making as well as sexual perversions. It is because of these acts that God sent the Great Deluge to wipe away all evidence of this knowledge.

There is a later echo of this imagery in Dante's *Inferno*. Once Dante and Virgil have passed through the Gates of Hell, but before they have reached the Acheron, Virgil explains to Dante about the apathetic angels:

> Heaven chased them out, so as not to become less beautiful, and the depths of Hell also rejected them, lest the evil might find occasion to glory over them (*canto* III).

Virgil tells Dante that in this liminal space – a place that is divorced from Hell, Purgatory or Paradise – 'the world does not remember them at all; mercy and justice treats them with contempt'.

In the Anglo-Norman *Voyage*, Brendan and his companions arrive at a Paradise of Birds and find a tall tree covered with birds, rising above the clouds. After Brendan prays for counsel, a bird descends to explain their apathy during Satan's fall and thus they are relegated to earth in the form of birds. This transformation is permanent in the *Voyage*. Conversely in the *Nauigatio* they only become birds on Sundays and on Holy Days; at other times they 'wander about in the air, the earth and the sky, like other spirits on their missions'.[35] Thus the angels' change in form in the *Nauigatio* echoes the respite of Judas Iscariot later in the narrative.

Benedeit's version shows that the angels were deceived and had obeyed a very clever master; thus God took pity on them and allowed them this Paradise between Heaven and Hell. However, the poet is censured for allowing the angels any amelioration of their fate and giving them permission to praise God. A manuscript in Lincoln College Oxford says that 'This is obviously contrary to Catholic belief. True belief holds that when the chief [that is, the chief of the rebel Angels, i.e., Lucifer] fell, none could have fallen with him unless they [too] were doomed.'[36] Whatever the power

---

[35] Selmer, *Nauigatio, caput* XII, ll. 41–44.
[36] Meyer, 'Satire en vers rythmiques', p. 378, ll. 26–29.

and the popularity of the Anglo-Norman *Voyage*, the author of this document felt it was necessary to speak out against the heresy of the neutral angels, and remind the audience that the only truth was that contained in the Bible: and that the neutral angels played no part in the divine plan.

This scene has been greatly abbreviated in comparison with the corresponding scene in the *Nauigatio* where the focus is on canonical hours and the lists of psalms. While there is a message of salvation in the Anglo-Norman *Voyage* – most particularly that the birds are allowed to worship God and draw comfort from the monks' presence – the shorter scene serves to maintain the momentum.

The war in heaven between Michael and Lucifer is described in the Middle English *South English Legendary*, a collection of saints' lives which also includes an abridged version of the Brendan legend. The oldest manuscript is MS Laud 108 (held in the Bodleian Library) which dates from 1280–90.[37] The legend of St Michael explains that there were once ten orders of angels and only a tenth fell with Lucifer, consequently mankind was created in order to replace those fallen angels (ll. 210–14). This legend also describes angels who were 'sumdel in mis-þouȝte' (somewhat in error) now live under the firmament in an earthly paradise awaiting Judgement Day when they will once again return to heaven. There is also a tradition that these neutral angels were 'elves' ('eluene' l. 255) or faerie folk.[38]

The concept of human souls or archangels represented

---

[37] Carl Horstmann, *The Early South English Legendary or lives of saints: 1, MS Laud, 108, in the Bodleian Library*, EETS OS 87 (London; N. Trübner & Co, 1887), p. x.

[38] See C.S. Lewis, *The Discarded Image* (Cambridge: Cambridge University Press, 1967), p. 136.

as birds also appears in the *Immrama*. In the *Voyage of Bran*, an ancient tree in blossom is filled with birds that sing the canonical hours; similarly in the *Voyage of Snedgus* there is a tree with beautiful birds, and a great bird tells of creation and Christ and the Last Judgement; the *Voyage of the Hui Corra* speaks of a bird flock of angels making music to the Lord; also, the Archangel Michael appears as a great bird, while one of the monks dies and reappears as a bird. The same text also mentions the souls that are released from Hell on a Sunday in the forms of birds.[39] This imagery is not restricted to the *Immrama:* in the *Vision of Adamnan* the souls of the righteous appear as 'pure white doves', whereas the souls of the wicked appear as ravens.

Curiously, *Immram curaig Máele Dúin* does not include an encounter with the soulbirds, although the travellers hear the distant singing of psalms and see an island full of birds.[40] The scene in *Máel Dúin* could be a condensed version of the comparable encounter in the *Nauigatio*, or perhaps in this *Immram*, the concept of a respite for the angels is so heretical that it was excluded from the text; indeed, it is also omitted from some of the versions of the Latin and Irish versions of the *Vita Brendani* which have been conflated with the voyage tales.

Christmas to Epiphany – The Community of Ailbe

After leaving the Paradise of Birds, the monks travel for four months to reach another island; however they have difficulty finding a landing spot. They circle the island 'until the sixth month' (l. 630). Once they land, they find two

---

[39] Stokes, 'Hui Corra', pp. 33, 42–45, 48–51.
[40] Stokes, 'Máel Dúin', p. 493.

The Anglo-Norman Voyage of St Brendan

springs but, despite their dehydration, they are ordered to wait until they know the nature of these springs. Thus, the approach to the monastic Community of Ailbe represents the monastic virtues of obedience and restraint. (The fact that the monks ignore this advice when they later reach a spring that induces sleep after they drink it suggests that the monks need to *experience* the temptation for themselves. They do not learn by cautions and maxims alone).

The brethren are approached by a 'tall, old man' whom they recognise because of his habit. He leads them to 'a good and fine abbey' which was founded by another Irish monk, St Ailbe of Emly, under whom these residential monks learned their monastic rules (l. 735). Here, the monks are held by a vow of silence; indeed, they do not allow the visitors to interrupt the holy office (in the way that the sinking island disturbs the Easter celebrations), their only expression is the divine office. Their monastic discipline ensures that the abbot waits until after the canonical hour has been sung before the abbot explains their circumstances to Brendan. The monks have lived on the island for 'eighty years since St Ailbe died'. Brendan is told that he and his brethren may stay until the Octave of Epiphany.

The Community of Ailbe represents monastic perfection. Benedeit depicts it as 'a good and fine abbey; there is no holier one beneath the firmament'. Thomas O'Loughlin describes it as a 'foretaste of heaven'.[41] There is, however, a contradiction between the monastic poverty, and the monks' expensive golden vestments and ornate reliquaries,

---

[41] Thomas O'Loughlin, 'Distant Islands: The Topography of Holiness in the *Nauigatio sancti Brendani*,' *The Medieval Mystical Tradition in England, Ireland and Wales*, ed. Marion Glasscoe (Cambridge: D.S. Brewer, 1999): 1–20, p.17.

even though these are in keeping with the Anglo-Norman customs of Benedeit's time.[42]

Miracles in the Community of Ailbe

The monks of the Community of Ailbe are sustained by what might be considered as three miracles; firstly, like Paul the Hermit in the penultimate episode of Brendan's voyage, these monks are exceptionally long-living: Brendan is told it is eighty years since St Ailbe died and since then the monks have suffered no sickness (l. 741). The second apparent miracle is the mysterious provision of food. The abbot explains that bread is brought to them each day – each loaf is shared by two monks. In addition, the Abbot anticipated the arrival of Brendan and his brethren because they received additional provisions on the day of their arrival.

The divine provision of food has parallels in the Bible from the Israelites receiving manna in the desert (Exodus 16; Numbers 11:6–9) or the ravens that bring food to Elijah (1 Kings 17:6). It is also seen again in the episode with Paul the Hermit. In both the *Nauigatio* and the Anglo-Norman version, Brendan's monks are given food by a mysterious messenger who ultimately guides the brethren to Paradise and the inference is that he may also be providing food for the Community of Ailbe, although the Abbot explains that he does not know the source of this bread (l. 743). This is different from the *Nauigatio* where the abbot explains that they receive their food 'by means of some dependent

---

[42] Carsten Wollin, 'The *Navigatio sancti Brendani* and Two of its Twelfth-Century Palimpsests: The Brendan Poems by Benedeit and Walter of Châtillon' in *The Brendan Legend: Texts and Versions*, ed. G.S. Burgess and Clara Strijbosch (Leiden: Brill, 2006): 281–313, p. 291.

creature' (*caput* XII), while a Middle English version relates that 'a straunge man eche daye it bringeth' (ll. 292, 294) without any further explanation. This also suggests that it is the messenger who provides it.

The final miracle is that the abbot explains how the lamps of the monastery 'lights on its own accord and it goes out on its own accord' (l. 761) using neither wax nor oil. Significantly, Brendan takes this statement at face value and does not ask to see this miracle for himself. In the *Nauigatio,* Brendan witnesses for himself how 'a fiery arrow sped through a window … and lit all the lamps that were placed before the altars' (*caput* XII). When Brendan questions how this is possible, the abbot describes this as spiritual light, equating it to the burning bush that Moses saw on Mount Sinai 'that bush was unaffected by the fire'.

Other Principal Encounters

The last encounters that appear in both the *Nauigatio* and Anglo-Norman *Voyage* are the most memorable. The brethren see a giant pillar in the sea which commentators have identified with an iceberg, but which are presented in religious terms. In the *Nauigatio* it is described in terms of the temple which appears Ezekiel (40–42). In the Anglo-Norman version, parallels can be drawn between the crystal pillar and the New Jerusalem of Revelation (21:19–21)

Silver columns also appear in *Immram curaig Ua Corra* and *Immram curaig Máele Dúin*. One of Máel Dúin's crew tears away a piece of a silver net on the column to offer on the altar of Armagh which might also act as some proof of the Otherworld to their homeland, whereas in the *Nauigatio* and the Anglo-Norman versions, Brendan takes a chalice from the pillar that will be used in their worship. For the Anglo-Norman version this corresponds to the golden goblet that one of the supernumeraries attempted to steal from the Deserted City.

Another natural feature that is presented in supernatural terms is the Smithy of Hell which has already been discussed in relation to the departure of one of the supernumeraries.

The arrival at the Smithy of Hell is one of the pivotal moments in the narrative: Brendan admits that he is not in control of their destiny. The presence of the demonic had the potential of creating a very real fear in the hearts of any audience. A secular audience may well have correlated the allegory of the demonic smith with the vivid Biblical descriptions of Hell and this may have shaken them into considering their own salvation. In the *Nauigatio*, the encounter at the Smithy of Hell avoids any overtly graphic descriptions, whereas in the Anglo-Norman *Voyage* Benedeit takes the opportunity to enhance the details and turn the encounter into a truly horrifying experience.

The embellished description of the island appeals to all senses through the thunderous roaring of the smith's bellows, the huge burning blades and the rocks (ll. 1128–33). Likewise, the emergence of the demon gives Benedeit the opportunity for an elaborate and terrifying description of a giant with flaming eyes, spewing fire and carrying a fiery blade similar to the Greek deity Hephaestus, the personification of fire. Benedeit then presents a series of destructive images to show how the monks face a very real threat: the missile hurled by the demon is described in terms of a sling-shot, a crossbow bolt and a whirlwind. The blade passes over the monks and falling into the sea, where it remains burning 'like heather in a clearing'. This simile would have probably been the most effective in conveying a message to a medieval audience: unless whipped into hysterical frenzy, the courtly audience would be unlikely to see a demon, whereas they would empathise with the fact that an uncontrolled fire could destroy property, crops or livestock and could be ruinous.

The encounter at the Smithy of Hell in the Anglo-Norman *Voyage* ends with the message that hardship in the service of God is ultimately rewarded. The use of horror in this version is not designed to terrify the courtly audience, but instead provides a safe environment for discussing issues that one would normally be unwilling to confront (in this case, damnation). The Anglo-Norman audience would believe neither that they were looking at the entrance to Hell, nor that they were facing damnation themselves. Instead, they experience the horror of the damnation through an empathy with the monk and a fear for his soul. However, they are also able to distance themselves from the events, as described below.

The Crystal Pillar and the fiery mountain would have been familiar to each audience through medieval geographers' writings, but these locations have been defamiliarised to give them a supernatural quality. The vagueness of description gives them an ethereal quality. The exotica are presented as two polarities with a series of oppositions: ice/fire, light/darkness, symmetrical/craggy, calm/fear, salvation/damnation. The damnation of the supernumerary shows that even among the brethren there is evil that must be excised before Paradise can be achieved.

The scenes with the Crystal Column and the Smithy of Hell serve to counterbalance each other. On the one hand, we have the column presenting a message of hope to each audience. With the descriptions echoing those of the New Jerusalem, the column is charged with positive Biblical symbolism. It is linked with the Otherworld through its association with apocryphal or classical symbolism and it concludes with a Christian mass, symbolising eternal life. On the other hand, the Smithy of Hell is a noisy and violent place, distinguished by its red and black colouring. The horrific descriptions are not dissimilar to the volcanic entrances to Hell as described by medieval geographers. The Smithy of Hell should be considered as such, especially with the damnation of the supernumerary. The passage from the Crystal Column, to the Smithy of Hell and then to the descriptions of Hell provided by Judas Iscariot, suggest a fall from salvation, which can only be arrested by the discipline as described by Paul the Hermit.

Judas Iscariot

Perhaps the most dramatic and memorable scenes in the *Voyage of Brendan* is the penultimate encounter before the brethren reach Paradise. Here, in the middle of the ocean, having fled the demon smithy and the loss of one of the supernumeraries at the shores of Hell, the brethren find a small rock with a man on it, beaten by the tempestuous waves. He is held there by two iron forks and a cloth which the wind whips so it strikes him across the eyes and face. Brendan asks who he is and what he had done to deserve such a punishment. The unfortunate explains that he is Judas Iscariot and that this is a comparative respite from Hell. In

The Anglo-Norman Voyage of St Brendan

the *Nauigatio* he explains that he receives a respite each Sunday and then at principal dates in the Christian calendar: Christmas to Epiphany; Easter to Pentecost, and on the feasts of the Purification and Assumption of the Virgin. Consequently, Judas's respite from Hell mirrors Brendan's own respite from the journey at the key locations where he celebrates these feasts. At other times, Judas explains, he burns 'like a lump of molten lead … in the centre of the mountain' where they lost one of the supernumeraries.

This scene is one of the principal differences between the *Nauigatio* and the Anglo-Norman *Voyage*. Benedeit has expanded this relatively short scene to approximately 250 lines, almost half of which are a description of the tortures. Scenes of violence are very few in the narrative, so when they come, they are graphic and terrifying. At the point in narrative that Judas recounts the story of the betrayal, he repeats the phrase 'when I saw' six times, equating to his six days of torture in Hell. He explains there are two Hells and he is the only one who suffers in both of them: the first Hell is on a mountain top; hot and sweaty and the more painful. The other Hell is in a valley, cold and stinking and the more horrible of the two; the two are separated by the sea.[43]

Brendan then asks Judas to explain the items that he has with him. Judas explains that he has a cloak which, during his lifetime, he gave the cloak to a leper, which saved him from dying in the sun; now it offers meagre protection from the elements as his intentions had been good. However, the cloth whips him around the face and eyes because he had originally stolen it, and it was not his to give

---

[43] J.S. Mackley, 'The Torturer's "Art" in the Judas episode of Benedeit's *Voyage of St Brendan*' in *Notes and Queries* 54.1 (April, 2007): 24–27.

away. The iron forks upon which the cloth hangs represent forks Judas gave to priests to support their cauldrons, and the priests now pray for him. Finally, the rock upon which Judas sits denotes a stone that he placed in a trench on a road, to act as a stepping-stone thus preventing travellers from straying some distance on their journey. (In the Anglo-Norman version, the rock has become a hillock, and there is the addition of a small strong bridge which suggests that Judas was indeed helping travellers to overcome a serious impediment on their journey). Thus, the suggestion is that no matter how heinous the overall sin, Christ rewards each good deed, in the same way that he punishes each sin.

Finally, Judas pleads with Brendan to intercede on his behalf and to secure for him a further day of respite; Brendan invokes the name of Christ to keep the devils away. The following day the demons complain that *they* have been tortured because they could not bring Judas back to Hell; they threaten to inflict double torture on Judas. Brendan tells them that they do not have the authority to do this, as he speaks in the name of Jesus Christ. The demons drag Judas away and Brendan continues on his journey.

This description of Judas's good deeds is not included in the Bible or its Apocrypha, nor is the concept of the day of respite from Hell. These ideas were likely developed in the earliest versions of the Brendan legend, known as the *Vita Dubliensis* (or VB3), where the monks complain to Brendan about travelling in hail and snow; they speculate that infernal regions could not be worse than the cold that they are enduring. Brendan berates them, alluding to another voyage, and explains:

We have seen Judas, the betrayer of our Lord, in a dreadful sea, on the Lord's day, wailing and lamenting, seated on a rugged and slimy rock, which was now submerged by the waves and again emerged from them somewhat. Against the rock there rushed a fiery wave from the east, and a wave of coldness from the west alternatively, which drenched Judas in a frightful manner; and yet this grievous punishment seemed to him a relief from pain, for thus the mercy of God granted this place to him on the Sundays as some ease amidst his torments. What, therefore, must be the torments suffered in Hell itself?[44]

As this version of the *Vita Brendani* is the only one to include the Judas episode in this form, Fr Denis O'Donoghue argues that this scene presents the earliest form of Brendan's encounter with Judas.[45] By alluding to an earlier voyage, Brendan's discussion of Hell glosses over the details, rather than have the monks and the audience witness them first hand; it also avoids being heretical by containing only the vaguest details concerning Judas's respite from Hell. Without descriptions of Judas's virtuous acts or Brendan's intercession, it lacks the moral effect of later versions of the legend. It cautions about the punishments of Hell without detailing them, instead creating an image of appalling weather conditions that the audience would recognise.

There is a short Irish text that borrows scenes from an Irish version of the *Vita* of Brendan entitled 'The Twelve Apostles of Ireland' which describes how a 'wonderful flower' from the Otherworld appears to the twelve Patriarchs: eventually, it is decided that Brendan should

---

[44] Patrick F. Moran, ed., *Acti Sancti Brendani: Original Latin Documents connected with the Life of Saint Brendan, Patron of Kerry and Clonfert* (Dublin: Kelly, 1872), p. 22.
[45] Denis O'Donoghue, *Lives and Legends of Saint Brendan the Voyager* (Felinfach: Llanerch, 1994), p. 243.

travel to find the land whence the flower came.[46]

On one occasion in the 'Twelve Apostles', the Devil appears on the mast of the monks' vessel: Brendan alone can see him. Brendan questions the Devil as to why he has 'come from Hell before his proper time'. The devil explains that he has come to be 'tortured in the deep prisons of this black dark sea.' Thus, this scene echoes the encounter with Judas that is seen in the *Nauigatio*, except that it is the devil that has been moved from his normal Hell, rather than Judas. The devil explains that no one can see Hell and survive, yet he still reveals it to Brendan. The 'Twelve Apostles' continues with an excessive list of monstrous descriptions of the torments after which Brendan hears helpless weeping at the bottom of Hell. On a huge rock, washed over by an infernal sea, Judas is hit by a wave of fire from the front and ice from behind. Judas explains that he will be tormented thus until Judgement Day. He does not repent of his sins; his message is against avarice and the 'despicable useless riches of the world'. Judas recounts some 'little verses' as a memorial for Brendan in which he explains that he 'died not ... I find not death but remain alive.' The text then ends abruptly.

Clearly, what survives of the 'Twelve Apostles' was not intended to be the full text: after the introductory scenes, one might speculate that Brendan was expected to travel to the Otherworld, to return with the wonderful flower and only be parted with it as the herald of his death in a manner akin to St Ailbe.[47] However, Séamus Mac Mathúna observes

---

[46] Published as 'Dá apstol décc na hÉrenn' in Charles Plummer, *Lives of the Irish Saints*, vol. 1, pp. 96–102, and in translation in vol. 2, 93–98.

[47] In the *Vita Ailbe*, Ailbe brings back the fruitful branch as testimony that he has travelled to the Otherworld. For the *Vita Ailbe*, see W.W. Heist, *Vitae*

that the Judas episode is what most interested the author of the 'Twelve Apostles' rather than the actual voyage.[48]

As the story developed, this episode represents another example of the liberal theology that is principally demonstrated by the author of the *Nauigatio*, but which is also conveyed in the Anglo-Norman Version; it is also shown in the episode with the neutral angels. Although Judas is tortured for his betrayal of Christ (and more importantly, his despair that he could not be forgiven), he also receives a comparative respite from Hell for the good deeds that he performed in his lifetime, although he is never truly away from it.

The concept of a day of respite may well have been influenced by the fourth century *Apocalypse of Paul*, an apocryphal text that is itself considered heretical. The text describes how Paul is taken to witness the judgements of the righteous and sinners, and the ensuing blessings and punishments. His grief and anguish at the torments in Hell is reflected in the Anglo-Norman version of the legend where Brendan laments Judas's fate.[49] However, in the *Apocalypse* an angel rebukes Paul, asking whether he is more merciful than God, and only when Christ appears in Hell do the sinners plead for 'refreshment', to which Jesus demands 'What *good* works have ye done?' Punishment is inflicted without mercy on those who had no mercy in their lifetime, yet, Jesus grants the sinners grace because of Paul's

---

sanctorum Hiberniae. Brussels: Société des Bollandistes, 1965, pp. 118–31; Cf. Eleanor Hull, 'The Silver Bough in Irish Legend,' 430–45.

[48] Séamus Mac Mathúna, 'The *Irish Life of Saint Brendan*: Textual History, Structure and Date,' *The Brendan Legend: Texts and Versions*, eds. Glyn S. Burgess and Clara Strijbosch (Leiden: Brill, 2006):117–58, p. 151 n. 87.

[49] 'Pur le parler Brandans ne pout/ Avant parler, mais dunc se tout.' (ll. 1267–8).

intercession for them. Thus, Brendan's function in the Judas episode is similar to that of Paul in the *Apocalypse*.

Ironically, the Judas episode presents a message of hope. On account of his good deeds, Judas is temporarily allowed to reach the threshold of Hell and look upon a world without infernal torment. However, despite his punishment being less severe on his days of respite, he is never truly away from it. Likewise, at the end of the episode, Brendan stands at the threshold of ending his seven year voyage and finally achieving Paradise. The Sunday respite may be a release and something to give Judas hope while he endures his suffering (although his suffering may be so intense he can think of nothing else), but it is also a further tantalising torture that he takes a frustrating step closer to salvation, but cannot go any further.

Paul the Hermit

Having met with Judas Iscariot, arguably the darkest aspect of humanity, Brendan's final encounter before reaching Paradise is with a hermit called Paul who is the antithesis of Judas. While, in the Bible, Judas was the treasurer of the apostles and appears still to be obsessed with possessions, Paul the Hermit has given up all material things, ultimately including clothing and food, to come closer to God. Consequently, the Anglo-Norman *Voyage* presents Paul as angelic in relation to Brendan. Paul represents the conflict between monasticism (the communal life) and eremitism (the solitary life). Paul serves God in his own contemplative way, but he is alone rather than part of a community. Brendan's monks survive by hard work, whereas Paul's continued existence depends first on an otter bringing him food and then on the spring of life-sustaining water.

The Anglo-Norman Voyage of St Brendan

Brendan's encounter with Paul the Hermit derives from the fourth-century *Vita Pauli* by Jerome.[50] In this *vita*, Paul is often considered to be the first hermit, who lives a life of prayer and penitence in the desert for most of his 113-year life, wearing only leaves or nothing at all. It is said that he survived by consuming only fruit and water. The legend also describes how a raven provided bread for him. This echoes the provision of food in the Community of Ailbe, but also emphasises that there is a physical presence to bring the food. Likewise, when Paul is visited by St Anthony, the raven brings a double portion of food.

Brendan would have recognised a Desert Father as an incontestable authority on the nature of salvation. As a hermit who had humbled himself before God, Paul makes Brendan feel that his own vow of abstinence is insufficient in comparison. The life of hardship that Paul endures equates to the difficulties that Brendan experiences on his journey. Even though Paul lives a life of abstinence, God, in his mercy, provides food and water as required, as well as hair that acts as clothing. In the same way, God supplies provisions for Brendan on his voyage. Paul, in his piety, is an appropriate figure to mirror Judas Iscariot and presents Brendan with the most holy of saints and the most heinous of sinners.

The *Nauigatio* (*caput* XXVI) gives more details concerning Paul's background and these have been changed from Jerome's *Vita Pauli* to appeal to an Irish audience. Paul explains that he lived in the service of the monastery of St Patrick for forty years. When Paul is digging a grave for

---

[50] Jacobus de Voragine, *Legenda Aurea*, ed. Thomas Graesse (Osnabrück: Otto Zeller Verlag, 1969), p. 95.

one of the brethren, the ghost of St Patrick appears and explains that he, Patrick, is to be buried in the place where Paul had planned to inter the brother. This is presumably so that no one would venerate the saint's grave. Patrick then commands Paul to live a solitary life. Paul then drifts in a boat for seven days (which equates to the seven years of Brendan's pilgrimage), until he arrives at the island that is to be his dwelling for the next eighty years, awaiting the day of his death. So, while Judas had been found on the threshold to Hell, Paul is encountered on the threshold to heaven.

In both versions, Paul demonstrates his eremitic perfection as he has given up *all* his worldly goods. The Anglo-Norman version describes him as naked and his body is only covered with hair (ll. 1535–36). In order to sustain himself, Paul drinks from a small 'cup-like' spring of water. Initially, Paul trusted in God to provide his nourishment: an otter walks on its hind legs carrying a fish (l. 1571).[51] However, by the time that Brendan encounters Paul, the Hermit no longer needs food to survive.

The Anglo-Norman *Voyage* omits any discussion of Paul's life in the monastery and the apparition that commanded him to become a hermit. In this version, Paul describes how, before he came to the life of isolation, he had lived in the world for fifty years and that, wishing to serve God, he had found a boat ready to travel (ll. 1555–56). Since arriving on the island, he has been free from pains and enjoyed eternal summer. He is confident that he

---

[51] See Glyn S. Burgess, 'The Use of Animals in Benedeit's Version of the Brendan Legend.' *The Brendan Legend: Texts and Versions*, eds. Glyn S. Burgess and Clara Strijbosch (Leiden: Brill, 2006): 11–34, pp. 23–24, 29. In the *Nauigatio*, the otter arrives at the hour of Nones, suggesting that even in the wilderness, Paul follows the monastic day.

will rise with the righteous because of the holy life that he has spent on the island (ll. 1566–68).

This scene has parallels in the *Immram curaig Máele Dúin* and the *Immram curaig Ua Corra*.[52] As with Brendan's voyage, Máel Dúin's meeting with the hermit is the penultimate episode of the tale. The hermit explains that an otter brought him an uncooked salmon; as the hermit could not eat raw flesh, the hermit threw it back into the sea. Later, the otter brings the salmon and a second brings smouldering firewood so that the hermit could cook the fish.[53]

For Brendan, the encounters with Judas and Paul represent the extremes of humanity. The horror of Judas's torment and damnation (which echoes the violence of the Smithy of Hell and the damnation of the supernumeraries) is contrasted with the tranquillity of Paul's anticipation of salvation (which also echoes the encounter at the crystal pillar). Similarly, Judas's need for God's mercy and a day of respite counterbalances Paul's wanting for nothing. Even though the two scenes are perfectly balanced to depict the extremes of humanity, they are also able to present Brendan in a central position to them both: Brendan wants for nothing, but only because of God's mercy.

The emphasis of these scenes is on the nature of sin and contrition. The lesson presented in both versions is clear: trust in God's mercy. By doing so, one may look forward to all the rewards that await the saints after their deaths. Some of these rewards are described when Brendan finally reaches the *Terra repromissionis sanctorum*, which is the ultimate destination of his seven-year journey.

---

[52] Stokes, 'Máel Dúin (suite),' pp. 80–91; Stokes, 'Húi Corra,' pp. 60–63.
[53] Stokes, 'Máel Dúin', pp. 88–89.

Paradise

The search for Paradise represents the search for an impossible perfection. In the Middle Ages it is embodied by the Holy Grail and also represented in both the *Nauigatio* and the Anglo-Norman version by the areas of the *Terra repromissionis sanctorum* (the Promised Land of the Saints) that Brendan cannot reach.[54]

After Brendan and his monks have heard the account of Paradise and learnt the lesson of absolute faith from Paul the Hermit, they are ready to see the *Terra repromissionis sanctorum*. The descriptions of Paradise in both the *Nauigatio* and the Anglo-Norman *Voyage* draw their imagery from writings about the Otherworld that would have been popular in the Middle Ages, for example through the Old English bestiaries and the poem of 'The Phoenix'. The 'delightful plateau' is an area, like the *Terra repromissionis sanctorum*, where there are no adverse weather conditions, there is a lingering scent of sweet perfume, and the land is 'abloom with delights'.[55] Authors who promulgated the descriptions of Paradise were consistent in the descriptions of the bounteous land, although there was some debate as to where the land was situated. Celtic mythology suggested that there was a Land to the West, or beyond a mist barrier, both of which are seen in versions of the Brendan narrative.[56]

---

[54] See, for example, A.C.L. Brown, *The Origins of the Grail Legend* (New York: Russell and Russell, 1966), p. 286.

[55] 'The Phoenix,' *The Exeter Anthology*, I, pp. 166–90. For further discussion see, for example, J.B. Allen and Daniel G. Calder, *Sources and Analogues of Old English Poetry: The Major Latin Texts in Translation* (Cambridge: D.S. Brewer Ltd., 1970), pp. 113–20. Dicuil describes the legend of the Phoenix as being Arabian in origin; see Tierney, *Liber de mensura orbis terrae*, p. 86.

[56] The mist barrier is also found in Norse and classical literature, see Howard Rollin Patch, *The Other World According to Descriptions in Medieval Literature*

The Anglo-Norman Voyage of St Brendan

Despite all the knowledge that the monks have gained during their seven-year purgatorial voyage, it is still not enough to achieve Paradise: the host has to guide them for the remainder of their journey (ll. 1632–33).[57] Paradise cannot be achieved by human qualities alone, but only with the guidance of God's representative.

As mentioned above, the barrier of mist is a common motif in Celtic mythology and passing through it is a means of reaching the Otherworld. This could suggest that the Otherworld borders the natural world and the boundaries are fluid. Of course, the *Nauigatio* also describes how Barrindus and Mernoc travel through the 'Gates of Paradise' (*Portam paradisi*, caput I, l. 72) and that they reach the Delightful Island (*insulam deliciosam*) where Mernoc dwells for a comparatively short time. With regard to the mist barrier, however, the Anglo-Norman *Voyage* is more explicit, declaring that the 'great fog blinds one so much, that whoever enters it loses his sight completely unless God gives him the vision' (ll. 1655–57). However, given that the emphasis of the Anglo-Norman *Voyage* is on the fact that Brendan and his monks have achieved spiritual enlightenment and find no fear in any of their encounters, the cloud barrier symbolically divides 'to the width of a street' and they no longer need to navigate in blindness (ll. 166).

Once in Paradise, Brendan discovers that time is suspended. The *Terra repromissionis sanctorum* is a place where time cannot be measured by human senses. The *Nauigatio*

(Cambridge, Mass.: Harvard University Press, 1950), pp. 20–21 and 44–46.
[57] There is a corresponding scene in *Máel Dúin* where Máel Dúin, approaching the island of the blessed, sees a rotating wall of fire which renders the island impervious without divine assistance, see Stokes, 'Máel Dúin (suite),' pp. 80–81.

describes how the journey through the mist barrier is *like* that of an hour, although one cannot accurately gauge the time (*caput* XXVIII, l. 10). Barrindus believed that he was there for only forty days, only to be told that he had existed a year without food or sustenance (*caput* I, ll. 57–58).[58] In addition, when Brendan is there, there is no alternation between day and night against which to measure time. The descriptions in the *Nauigatio* are only curtailed when the monks reach an impassable river. However, Brendan is unperturbed that he cannot go any further, simply stating that 'we must remain ignorant of the size of this country' (*caput* XXVIII, ll. 19–20). Here Brendan is similar to Moses, who is unable to cross the river Jordan (Deuteronomy 34:4).

The discovery of Paradise in the two versions of the Brendan narrative represents the quest for the boundaries of human knowledge. Even having achieved the *Terra repromissionis sanctorum*, Brendan must still shed his 'sinful' physical body before being allowed to witness the marvels that lie beyond the river. Thus, in the *Nauigatio*, just as Brendan did not witness Hell for himself, but simply stopped at the shore, so he cannot see the full extent of Paradise. The Anglo-Norman *Voyage* suggests that his understanding is limited by his physical mind (ll. 1793–94). However, despite the restrictions of Brendan's human understanding, the river also represents an assurance that Paradise awaits Brendan after death. The accounts of his

---

[58] In the *Immram Brain maic Febuil*, time is also abstract: the narrator explains that, when they reach the Island of Women, 'It seemed a year to them that they were there, but it chanced to be many years'. Similarly when Bran arrives at Srub Brain, he is told 'the Voyage of Bran is in our ancient stories,' §§62 and 64.

experiences will lead others to the saintly life.[59]

From a stylistic point of view, the description of Paradise in the *Nauigatio* is weak and brings the narrative to an anticlimactic end: the *Nauigatio* had already revealed the imagery of laden trees and precious stones in the narrative of Barrindus. Similarly, the abbot told Brendan that he and Mernoc were unable to cross the river that divides Paradise. Thus, as Waters observes, the author of the *Nauigatio* 'foolishly exhausted his ideas on this subject at the beginning of his work'.[60]

Unlike the author of the *Nauigatio*, Benedeit avoids revealing too much about the *Terra repromissionis sanctorum* early in the narrative. Thus the descriptions of Paradise come as a surprise to the audience. For example, the vivid colours of the flowers suggest that such beauty is accessible only to the pious. The narrative makes clear that it is only 'with the permission of the Divine King' that they are able to approach Paradise (l. 1649). The Anglo-Norman *Voyage* explains that this was the land where Adam was master, but to which he cannot return. Yet the descriptions are like the 'land of milk and honey' described in Exodus (ll. 1755–57; Exodus 3:8). Most particularly, for the Anglo-Norman *Voyage*, this is a reworking of the New Jerusalem in Revelation. The first feature of Paradise that the monks see is a wall, built up to the clouds, a reflection of Revelation 21:12–20. The architectural perfection suggests that the citadel has been divinely made of many precious stones: 'everything was in one piece, without incisions, there was no labour making it' (ll. 1683–84). The brethren are greeted by

---

[59] Burgess, '*Savoir* and *faire*,' p. 272.
[60] Waters, *Voyage*, pp. xcvii–xcviii.

a youth who calms the dragons that guard the gates of Paradise and makes them lie on the ground. He also causes the flaming swords to stop whirling, like Christ calming the seas (ll. 1727–28). In the same way that the darkness of the Deserted Citadel and the fog surrounding the *Terra repromissionis sanctorum* represent spiritual disorientation, the absence of any visual impairment shows that the monks are finally able to focus solely on God.

After an apparently short amount of time, during which the monks see many things, they finally see Paradise itself in the distance. Benedeit situates Paradise atop a mountain, which Jones argues is 'predictable', as it shows that in the Anglo-Norman *Voyage* 'assistance for the travellers always comes from above'.[61] In addition to the detailed descriptions of the bounteous land, there are also 'wonder-ful sights for which there is no explanation', as well as the visions of Paradise and the angels' divine singing being beyond the monks' human comprehension (ll. 1789–90). Indeed, it is not a physical barrier, which prevents Brendan from reaching Paradise, but the youth who guides them explains that Brendan possesses 'too little knowledge for this' (l. 1794). Thus, with the prediction that Brendan will soon return here in spirit, the youth tells them to return home, taking precious stones 'as tokens of their comfort' (l. 1806).

Given that the nature of the *Nauigatio* is more ecclesiastical than that of the Anglo-Norman *Voyage*, it is curious that the imagery of the former appears to be based on the Celtic Otherworld, whereas in the Anglo-Norman *Voyage* it is based on the New Jerusalem of Revelation. This

---

[61] Robin F. Jones, 'The Mechanics of Meaning in the Anglo-Norman *Voyage of Saint Brendan*,' *Romanic Review* 71 (1980): 105–13, p. 111.

could be because Barrindus, who originally describes Paradise in the *Nauigatio*, could be an echo of a Celtic deity.[62] Conversely, Benedeit may have used the imagery from Revelation and the whirling sword from Genesis to provide authority to his narrative, although the descriptions of the woods full of deer, gold and treasure houses would no doubt further appeal to the Anglo-Norman courtly audience.

Although the portrayals of Paradise in both versions describe the ideal for each audience and appeal to their basic needs (favourable weather conditions and an abundance of food) the depictions are dependent upon details in the Bible or classical works. In order to keep some of the divine mysteries intact, the final *Terra repromissionis sanctorum* is hidden from Brendan. In addition, the lack of description and the promise of what lies beyond the river, or in the Paradise on the mountain, suggests that the rewards for the righteous, when they finally achieve Paradise, will be much greater (ll. 1759–72 and 1797–78).

The return home

After Brendan has witnessed the mysteries of the ocean and seen as much of Paradise as the human mind can understand, both versions describe how Brendan and his brethren return home to Ireland. This return to Ireland brings a closure to the narrative. The inclusion of the return journey ensures that the voyage is not considered as a quest – simply seeking Paradise – but a pilgrimage, whereby Brendan can return home and bear witness to the marvels that he has seen on his journey.

---

[62] A.C.L. Brown, 'Barintus,' *Revue celtique* 22 (1901): 339–44, p. 341; cf. Selmer, *Nauigatio*, *caput* I, ll. 15–60.

Conclusion

The Anglo-Norman version of the *Voyage of Brendan* builds on the popularity of its Latin source material, the *Nauigatio sancti Brendani abbatis*. The author of the Latin original, which was composed between 795 and 950, had an extensive knowledge of Saints' Lives (most notably the *Vita* of Brendan), Biblical Apocrypha (particularly the book of Enoch and the Apocalypse of Paul), Irish Voyage Tales (*echtrae* and *immrama*) and the *Marvels of the East* as well as geographies such as Dicuil's *Liber de mensura orbis terrae* ('On the Measurement of the Earth').

In its various versions, the *Voyage of Brendan* provided exemplar of monastic living and the rewards of faith, as well as a chance to examine sensitive issues such as the nature of salvation and damnation and some of the encounters might serve to scare the complacent into contrition. There were those who disagreed with the liberal theology presented in the *Voyage of Brendan*, especially for those who had transgressed against God, but the punishment for these transgressors was not as severe as might be suggested in other didactic writings. Instead, the message was of God's infinite love and mercy for all, but especially the rewards for the faithful. In addition, there was the message concerning the search for the divine and transcending human limitations, all presented in an exciting adventure narrative.

The *Nauigatio* and the Anglo-Norman versions were composed for very different reasons. While the *Nauigatio* was a movement away from the details of the pious life found in the *Vita Brendani*, its focus was still based around the principal Christian festivals with a concentration on the monastic hours. Its function was primarily devotional and didactic. Conversely, the Anglo-Norman *Voyage* was written in octosyllabic rhyming couplets, and while it still contained religious themes, it was reworked into an exciting adventure with romance elements and marvellous imagery, aimed at a secular courtly audience, while at the same time presenting descriptions of monastic pilgrimages and seafaring.

Likewise, Benedeit removed the long lists of psalms and the excessively ecclesiastical nature of the narrative. On the other hand, the Anglo-Norman *Voyage* contains some of the earliest recognisable elements of romance in Old French literature, long before the development of romance as a genre. The *Nauigatio* was already widely disseminated. Through the Anglo-Norman *Voyage* presented the story in an original, exciting and innovative way and was the first of many vernacular translations. This goes some way towards explaining why the *Voyage of Brendan* was one of the most popular of the medieval narratives.

Manuscripts of the Anglo-Norman *Voyage*

London, British Library, Cotton Vespasian B.x, ff. 1r–11r (MS A).

This is the most complete version of the Anglo-Norman *Voyage*, omitting only six lines. The manuscript consists of twenty three vellum folios This manuscript of the *Voyage* dates from the beginning of the fourteenth century (although it is a copy of a twelfth-century manuscript) and is bound with texts including the *Nauigatio sancti Brendani*, a treatise claiming to be by Merlin and a treatise on cosmography translated into Latin by St Jerome.

Paris, Bibliothèque Nationale de France, nouv. Acq. fr. 4503, ff. 19v–42r (MS B).

The manuscript comprises seventy four vellum folios and dates from around 1200; 169 lines have been omitted, most of these from the last 300 lines; however two additional lines have been added; the other texts in the manuscript are hagiographic and religious writings.

Oxford, Bodleian Library, Rawlinson D 913, f. 85 (MS C).

This is a single vellum folio dating from the first half of the thirteenth century. It covers the first 310 lines of the text as shown by Waters' edition. Much of ll. 35–104 is illegible as it is likely that this folio was used as binding for another manuscript.

York, Minster Library Archives, XVI, K, 12 (I), ff. 23r–36r (MS D).

This manuscript dates from the first half of the thirteenth century. Unlike the other manuscripts that have been bound with religious writings, this manuscript collection includes a group of fables by Marie de France and another, unknown, author. Waters describes the work of this scribe as 'hasty and careless' which led to a 'large number of gross grammatical, metrical and other blunders'. Many of the lines have too many or too few syllables. However, he does acknowledge that the manuscript preserves some useful foundations of the critical text where other manuscripts (for example, MS A and B) fail.

Paris, Bibliothèque de l'Arsenal, 3516, ff. 96r–100v (MS E).

As with the York manuscript, this is a collection of secular material covering a total of 356 vellum folios. The *Voyage* has been rewritten, and the Anglo-Norman forms have been replaced by thirteenth century continental French with some Picard dialect. This manuscript was once illustrated with many miniatures of excellent quality. Although these have since been removed, it does suggest that this was a decorative manuscript for the enjoyment of the wealthy, rather than a functional manuscript to be read in church.

Cologny-Genève, Fondation Martin Bodmer, 17 (MS F).

This is the oldest surviving manuscript, dating from the twelfth century. It comprises four single-column folios of parchment containing just 131 lines (ll. 794–893, 1169–85, and 1188–206).

Episodes in the *Nauigatio*

1. Brendan's heritage and the story of Barindus
2. Brendan chooses his Companions
3. Brendan visits Enda
4. The Construction of the Coracle
5. The Three Late-coming Monks
6. The Uninhabited Island
7. The Stolen Bridle
8. The Messenger
9. The Island of Sheep
10. Jasconius
11. The Paradise of Birds
12. The Community of Ailbe
13. The Intoxicating Spring
14. The Coagulated Sea
15. The Celebration of the Festivals
16. The Fight of the Fish
17. The Island of the Three Choirs
18. The Island of the Grapes
19. The Fight of the Birds
20. Second Visit to the Community of Ailbe
21. The Transparent Sea and the Wonders of the Ocean
22. The Crystal Pillar
23. The Smithy of Hell
24. The Death of a monk
25. Judas Iscariot
26. Paul the Hermit
27. The Celebration of the Festivals
28. The *Terra repromissionis sanctorum*
29. Brendan's Return and Death

The Anglo-Norman Voyage of St Brendan

Episodes in the Anglo-Norman *Voyage*

1. Prologue and Dedication
2. Saint Brendan and his desire to see the Other World
3. The Narrative of Barrind
4. Brendan chooses Fourteen Companions
5. Preparations for the Voyage
6. The Three Intruding Monks
7. The First Voyage
8. The Uninhabited City
9. The Stolen Goblet
10. God provides all necessities
11. The Isle of Sheep
12. The Great Fish
13. The Paradise Of Birds
14. Preparations For The Second Year
15. The Isle of Ailbe
16. The Intoxicating Spring
17. Friends Revisited
18. The Fight of the Sea-Serpents
19. The Voyagers Are Miraculously Fed
20. Griffin versus Dragon
21. The Congregation of Sea Monsters
22. The Great Pillar and Canopy
23. The Smithy of Hell
24. The Smoke-capped Mountain
25. Judas Iscariot
26. A Monk Mysteriously Disappears
27. Paul the Hermit
28. The End of the Seventh Year
29. Paradise
30. Brendan's Return and Death

A note on the translation

This translation is, where possible, a line by line translation to assist with reading the Anglo-Norman. A more literary translation is to be found in Glyn Burgess's edition in *The Voyage of St Brendan: Representative Versions of the Legend in English Translation*, eds. W.R.J. Barron and Glyn S. Burgess, (Exeter: University of Exeter Press, 2002; 2nd Revised edition 2005): 65–102.

The Anglo-Norman
Voyage of St Brendan

Incipit Vita Sancti Brendani

Donna Aaliz la reïne,[1]
Par qui valdrat lei divine,
Par qui creistrat lei de terre[2]
E remandrat tante guerre,
Por les armes Henri lu rei,   5
Par le cunseil qui ert en tei
Salüet tei mil e mil feiz
Li apostoiles danz Benedeiz.
Que comandas, ço ad enpris,
Secund sun sens en letre mis,   10
En letre mis e en romanz
Esi cum fud li teons cumanz,
De saint Brendan le bon abeth.
Mais tul defent ne seit gabeth,
Quant dit que set e fait que peot: 15
Itel servant blasmer ne steot;
Mais cil qui peot e ne voile,
Dreiz est que cil mult s'en doile.

---

[1] Adeliza, wife to Henry I, and daughter of Duke Godfrey VII of Louvain. In MS *C* the name of the patroness is 'Mahalt'.
[2] 'Lei de terre,' for a discussion of the use of 'terre' in the Anglo-Norman Voyage of St Brendan see Glyn S. Burgess, 'Les fonctions des quatre éléments dans le *Voyage de saint Brendan* par Benedeit.' *Cahiers de Civilisation Médiévale X^e–XIIe siècles* 38 (1995): 3–22, p. 5.

The Anglo-Norman Voyage of St Brendan

Prologue and dedication

Here begins the life of St Brendan

My lady Adeliza the queen,
Through whom divine law will prevail
Through whom terrestrial law will grow stronger
And the great war will be brought to an end
Under the banner of Henry the king
Through the wise council that will be in you
The missioner Dom Benedeit)
Greets you a thousand and a thousand times.)
That which you commanded, this he has undertaken,
He has put into words to the best of his ability
Into writing and the Romance tongue[3]
As was your command
[The story] of St Brendan, the good abbot.
But you should preserve [the author] from being derided
When he says what he knows and does what he can:
Such a servant must not be blamed;
But it is right that the one who is capable and unwilling)
Should suffer much.[4])

---

[3] Benedeit claims that he is a translator; cf. M. Dominica Legge, '*Letre* in Old French,' *Modern Language Review* 56 (1961): 333–34.

[4] The dedication is summarised in MS *E* as 'Seignor oies que io dirai Dun saint home vos conterai Dyrlande estoit brandans ot non Molt ert de grant religion,' Paris, Bibliothèque de l'Arsenal 3516, fo. 96 r°. For a discussion of the dedication see C.R. Sneddon, 'Brendan the Navigator: A Twelfth-Century View,' *The North Sea World in the Middle Ages,* eds Thomas R. Liszka and Lorna E.M. Walker (Dublin: Four Courts Press, 2001): 211–29, pp. 224–25.

Icist seinz Deu fud ned de reis
De naisance fud des Ireis;   20
Pur ço que fud de regal lin,
Pur oc entent a noble fin.
Ben sout que la scripture dit:
'Ki de cest mund fuit le delit,
Od Deu de cel tant en avrat   25
Que demander plus ne savrat.'
Pur oc guerpit cist reials eirs
Les fals honurs pur iceals veirs–
Dras de moine–pur estre vil
En cest secle cum en eisil.   30
Prist e l'ordre e les habiz,
Puis fud abes par force esliz.
Par art de lui mult i vindrent
Qui al ordre bein se tindrent:
Tres mil suz lui par divers leus 35
Munies aveit Brandan li pius,
De lui pernanz tuz ensample
Par sa vertud que ert ample.

Saint Brendan

This saint of God was born of kings
Born of Ireland;
Because he was of royal line,
Because of this he strove for a noble purpose.
He knew well what the scriptures say:
'He who shuns the delights of this world,
Will have so many with God in heaven
That he could not ask for more.'[5]
On this account, this royal heir abandoned
False honours for the true ones –
Monk's habits – to be humble
In this worldly life as in exile.
He took both the orders and the habit,
And then he was perforce chosen to be an abbot.
Because of his skill many came there
Who observed the orders well:
Brendan the holy had three thousand
Monks under him from different places,
All taking their example from him
Because of his virtue which was great.

---

[5] Waters observes that, while the quotation does not correspond with any Biblical passage, the idea frequently occurs in the Gospels, for example, Matthew 6:19–21.

Li abes Brendan prist en purpens,
Cum hoem qui ert de mult grant sens,   40
De granz cunseilz e de rustes,
Cum cil ert forment justes,
De Deu prïer ne faiseit[6] fin
Pur sei e pur trestut sun lin,
E pur les morz e pur les vifs–   45
Quer a trestuz eret amis;
Mais de une ren li prist talent,
Dunt Deu prïer prent plus suvent,
Que lui mustrast cel paraïs
U Adam fud primes asis,   50
Icel qui est nostre heritét
Dun nus fumes deseritét.
Bien creit qu'ileoc ad grant glorie,
Si cum nus dit veire storie,
Mais nepurant voldret vetheir   55
U il devreit par dreit setheir,
Mais par peccét Adam forfist,
Pur quei e sei e nus for mist.
Deu en prïet tenablement
Cel lui mustret veablement;   60
Ainz qu'il murget voldreit saveir
Quel sed li bon devrunt aveir,
Quel u li mal aveir devrunt,
Quel merite il recevrunt;

---

[6] Short and Merrilees have *ferait* for Waters' *faiseit*, which seems more appropriate.

The Anglo-Norman Voyage of St Brendan

His desire to see the other world

The abbot Brendan resolved,
Like a man who had much good sense,
Of good and sound counsel,
Like one who is very righteous
That he would make relentless prayers to God
For himself and all his lineage
Both for the living and the dead –
For he was a friend of everyone;
But there was one thing which he particularly desired
For which he began to pray to God more frequently
That He should show him that Paradise
Where Adam was first seated
That which is our heritage
And from which we were disinherited.
He truly believes that there is great glory
And as the true history tells us[7]
But nevertheless he wanted to see
Where he ought by right to sit
But Adam forfeited by his sins
And in this way he put himself and us outside.
He prayed to God about it persistently
That He would show him Paradise for his own eyes;[8]
Before he died he wanted to know
What abode the good people were due to have
What place the wicked were due to have
What reward they will receive,

---

[7] 'Holy Scripture'.
[8] Literally, 'visibly'.

Enfern prïed vetheir oveoc,   65
E quels peines avrunt ileoc
Icil felun qui par orguil
Ici prennent par eols escuil
De guerreer Deu e la lei,
Ne entre eols nen unt amur ne fai.   70

Iço dunt lui pris est desir
Voldrat Brandans par Deu sentir.
Od sei primes cunseil en prent
Qu'a un Deu serf confés se rent:
Barinz out nun cil ermite,   75
Murs out bons e sainte vitte;
Li fedeilz Deu en bois estout,
Tres cenz moines od lui i out;
De lui prendrat conseil e los,
De lui voldrat aveir ados.   80
Cil li mustrat par plusurs diz,
Beals ensamples e bons respiz,
Qu'il vit en mer e en terre[9]
Quant son filiol alat querre:
Ço fud Mernoc, qui ert frerre   85
Del liu u cist abes ere,
Mais de ço fud mult voluntif,
Que fust ailurs e plus sultif.
Par sun abeth e sun parain.

---

[9] For a discussion of the use of 'eau', 'occean' and 'mer' see Burgess, 'quatre éléments,' p. 9; see also Jean Larmat, 'L'Eau dans la *Navigation de Saint Brandan* de Benedeit,' *L'Eau au Moyen Age*, Senefiance 15 (Aix-en-Provence: CUER MA, 1985).

He wanted to see Hell as well
And what torments will suffer there
Those wicked people who because of their pride
Here on their own accord rush
To wage war on God and the law
And who among themselves have neither love nor faith.

The Narrative of Barrind

This thing which he has come to desire
Brendan wishes to hear from God.
But first before taking a decision
He goes to a servant of God to make his confession:
The name of this hermit is Barrind,
He has a good way of living and a saintly life.[10]
The faithful servant of God lives in a wood,
He has three hundred monks there with him;
From him he [Brendan] will take counsel and advice,
From him he wants to have support.
This man shows him in many words
Fine parables and good maxims
Which he saw at sea and on land
When he went to look for his god-son:
This was Mernoc, who was a brother
In the place where Barrind was abbot,
But he was very desirous of that
Which was elsewhere and more solitary.
With the help of his abbot and his godfather

---

[10] Discussed in Brown, 'Barintus,' 339–44; cf. Béroul, *The Romance of Tristran*, trans. Norris J. Lacy (New York and London: Garland Publishing Inc., 1989), ll. 1360–1422.

En mer se mist, e nun en vain,[11]   90
Quer puis devint en itel liu
U nuls n'entret fors sul li piu:
Ço fud en mer en un' isle
U mals orrez nuls ne cisle,
U fud poüz de cel odur   95
Que en paraïs gettent li flur;
Quer cel' isle tant pres en fud,
U sainz Mernoc esteit curud,
De paraïs out la vie
E des angeles out l'oïde.   100
E pius Barinz la le requist,
U vit iço qu'a Brandan dist.

Quant ot Brandan la veüe
Que cist out la receüe,
De meilz en creit le soen conseil,   105
E plus enprent sun apareil.
De ses munies quatorze eslit,
Tuz le meilurs que il i vit,
E dit lur ad le soen purpens;
Savrat par eols si ço ert sens.   110
Quant oïrent iço de lui,
Dunc en parlerent dui e dui;

---

[11] Waters observes that no manuscript offers an entirely satisfactory reading to this problematic line. Burgess translates it as 'he had set sail on a mission, which turned out well'.

He put to sea, and not in vain,
For then he came to such a place
Where none can enter other than the pious:
It was at sea on an island
Where evil winds never howl,
Where it was fed with this perfume
Which the flowers emit in Paradise;
For this island was so near,
Where Saint Mernoc had sailed,
That from there Paradise could be seen
And the angels could be heard[12]
And saintly Barrind sought him out there
Where he saw that which he told Brendan.

Brendan chooses fourteen companions

When Brendan had heard of the sight
That the latter had received there[13]
The more he believed his advice,
And the more he began his preparations.
He selected fourteen of his monks,
The very best that he saw there[14]
And told them of his idea;
He wants to know from them if this is a wise course of
    action.
When they heard this from him
Then they talked about it in pairs;

---

[12] ll. 99–100. literally translated as 'Of Paradise there was sight/ And of angels there was hearing.'
[13] Burgess: 'When he had heard what Barint had seen there, Brendan
[14] Burgess: 'Those he saw to be the best'.

Respundent lui comunalment
Que ço enprist mult vassalment;
Prïerent l'en ques meint od sei   115
Cum les seons filz soürs en fei.
Ço dist Brandan: ' Pur cel vos di
Que de vos voil ainz estre fi
Que jo d'ici vos en meinge,
Al repentir puis m'en prenge.'   120
Cil promettent suurance
Pur eols ne seit demurance.

    Dunc prent l'abes iceols esliz,
Puis que out oït d'els tuz les diz,
En capitle les ad menez,   125
Iloc lur dit cum hoem senez:
'Seignurs, ço que en pensed avum,
Cum el est gref nus nel savum,
Mais prium Deu que nus enseint,
Par sun plaisir la nus en meint;   130
E enz el nun al saint Espirit
Juine faimes que la nus guit,
E junum la quarenteine
Sur les treis jurs la semaine.'
Dunc n'i ad nul qui se target   135
De ço faire qu'il lur charget
Ne li abes ne nuit ne jurn
Des ureisuns ne fait tresturn,
De ci que Deus li enveiat
Le angele del cel, quil aveait   140

The Anglo-Norman Voyage of St Brendan

They reply to him one and all[15]
That he should undertake this very boldly
They beseeched him to take them with him
As his own sons, secure in faith.
Brendan said the following: 'I tell you this
That I would sooner be certain of you
Than take you away from here
And then be obliged to repent of having done so.'
They gave an assurance
That they would not hinder him.

    Then the abbot takes these chosen ones
And when he had heard what they all had to say
He has led them all into the chapter house,
There he tells them as a prudent man:
'Gentlemen, what we have in mind,
How difficult it is we do not know[16]
But let us pray to God to instruct us,
At his pleasure he will lead us there;
And in the name of the Holy Spirit
We shall fast that he should guide us there
And we shall fast for forty days
On three days each week.'
Thus there is not one who delays
From doing that which he charges them
Nor does the abbot by night or day
Cease his prayers
Until God sent to him
The angel of heaven who would guide him

---

[15] Burgess: 'They all responded as one'.
[16] Benedeit, *Anglo-Norman Voyage*, ll. 127–28: 'We have no idea how difficult what we have envisaged is'.

De tut l'eire cum il irat;
Enz en sun quer sil aspirat
Que tres bein veit e certement
Cum Deus voldrat seon alement.
Dunc prent cungé a ses freres,   145
As quels il ert mult dulz peres,
E dit lur ad de seon eire
Cument a Deu le volt creire,
A sun priur tuz les concreit,
Dit lui cument guarder le deit;   150
Cumandet eals lui obeïr,
Cum lur abet mult bein servir.
Puis les baiset Brandan e vait.
Plurent trestuit par grant dehait
Que mener ne volt lur peres   155
Fors quatorze de lur freres.

Vait s'en Brandan vers la grant mer
U sout par Deu que dout entrer.
Unc ne turnat vers sun parent:
En plus cher leu aler entent.   160
Alat tant quant terre dure,
Del sujurner ne prist cure;
Vint al roceit que li vilain
Or apelent Salt Brandan. [17]

---

[17] 'Le Salt Brandan'. This is a mistranslation of 'Saltus uirtutis Brendani', which, in the *Nauigatio*, refers to Brendan's meadow, see Selmer, *Nauigatio*, *caput* I, l. 5. (This comes from the Irish 'Cluain-ferta Brenainn'). Waters observes that the Old French *salt*, *saut*, means 'leap' or 'projecting rock', and Benedeit seems to have used the example that one also sees in Béroul's

Throughout the journey he was to make[18]
Deep in his heart [the angel] so inspired him
That he saw very well and surely
That God wanted him to go.
Then he takes leave of his brethren
To whom he was a very kind father
And tells them about his journey
How he wishes to entrust it to God.
He commends them all to his prior
Telling him how he must look after them;
He commands them to obey him,
And serve him as if he were their abbot.
Then Brendan kisses them and departs.
They all weep with great dismay
That their father does not wish to take
More than fourteen of their brothers.

Preparations for the voyage

Brendan goes off towards the great sea
Where he knows from God that he must embark
Never did he turn towards his family
He is intent upon going to a more worthy place.
He went to the furthest point of land
He had no despire of staying put;
He came to the rock which the peasants
Now call Brendan's Leap.

Tristan, 'Encor claimant Coreualan/ Cele Pierre le Saut Tristan' (ll. 953–4); cf. Waters, *Voyage*, p. 102.

[18] Short and Merrilees suggest that this angel is the host who provides provisions for the brethren on their journey.

Icil s'estent durement luin 165
Sur l'occean si cume un gruign,
E suz le gruign aveit un port
Par un la mer receit un gort,
Mais petiz ert e mult estreit–
Del derube veneit tut dreit. 170
Altres, ço crei, avant cestui
Ne descendit aval cel pui.
Ci alloeces fist atraire
Mairen dunt sa nef fist faire,
Tute dedenz de fust sapin, 175
Defors l'avolst de quir bovin;
Uindre la fist que sculante
Od l'unde fust, e curante;
Ustilz i mist tant cum estout,
E cun la nef porter en pout; 180
La guarisun i mist odveoc
Qu'il aveient portét iloec,
Ne plus que a quarante dis
De viande n'i out enz mis.

Dist as freres: 'Entrez enenz. 185
Deu gracïez, bons est li venz.'[19]
Enz entrent tuit e il aprés.
Ast vos ja tres curanz adés,

---

[19] For a discussion concerning the term 'vent' see Burgess, 'Les fonctions des quatre éléments,' p. 14

The Anglo-Norman Voyage of St Brendan

This extends exceedingly far
Out into the ocean just like a groyne[20]
And on this groyne there was a haven
Through which the sea receives a stream,
But it was small and very narrow -
It came straight down from the cliff.
No others, this I believe, before this man
Had gone down this hill.
To this spot he had dragged
Timber from which he had his ship built,
Everything inside was made of pinewood,
The outside was covered with ox hide;
He had it caulked so that it was smooth-running
In the waves, and swift;[21]
He put gear in there as was necessary
And as much as the ship could carry;
He put provisions there as well
Which they had carried there,
No more than for forty days supply
Of food he had put therein.

The Three intruding monks

He said to the brothers: 'Come on board.
Give thanks to God, the wind is favourable.'
They all climb on board and he boards afterwards.
Behold now three running forthwith

---

[20] 'Gruign': Waters translates this (in this instance) as snout. Burgess uses the term 'promontory' for its appearance here and in l. 167.
[21] For a description of the construction of the coracle in the *immrama* see Stokes, 'Húi Corra,' pp. 38–41.

A haltes voiz Brandan criant
E lor palmes vers lui tendant: 190
'De ton muster sumes meüd
E desque ci t'avum seüd.
Lai nus, abes, a tei entrer,
E od tei, donz, par mer errer.'
Il les cunut e sis receit;   195
Qu'en avendrat, bien le purveit.
Ço que par Deu l'abes purvit
Ne lur celet, ainz lur ad dit:
'Les dous de vus avrat Satan
Od Abiron e od Dathan.   200
Li tierz de vus mult ert temptez,
Mais par Deu ert bien sustentez.'

Quant out ço dit l'abes Brandans,
Dunc drechet sus ambes les mains,
E Deu prïet escordement   205
Les seons fetheilz guard de turment;
E puis levet sus la destre,
Tuz les signet li sainz prestre.
Drechent le mast, tendent le veil,
Vunt s'en a plain li Deu fetheil.   210

Shouting to Brendan with a loud voice
And holding out the palms of their hands towards him:
'From your monastery we have departed
And we have followed you as far as here.
Let us, abbot, board with you
And voyage with you, lord, on the sea.'[22]
He knows them and receives them on board;
He foresees clearly what will befall as a result.
What, through God, the abbot foresaw
He did not hide from them, thus he spoke to them:
'Two of you Satan will have
With Abiram and Dathan.[23]
The third one of you will be greatly tempted
But will be well supported by God.'

The First voyage

When the abbot Brendan had said this
Then he raised up both his hands
And prayed to God with all his heart
To preserve his faithful servants from storms;[24]
And then he raised up his right hand
And blessed them all, the holy priest.
They raise the mast, spread the sail,
And go off smoothly, God's faithful servants.

---

[22] Cf. Stokes, 'Máel Dúin,' pp. 460–1; Stokes, 'Húi Corra,' pp. 38–39; Béroul, *The Romance of Tristran*, ll. 1708–10, 4040–42 and 4472–73.

[23] Cf. Numbers 16.

[24] Burgess: 'torment' rather than 'storms'. See his discussion in Glyn S. Burgess, 'La Souffrance et le repos dans *Le Voyage de saint Brendan* par Benedeit,' *Miscellanea Mediaevalia: Mélanges offerts à Philippe Ménard*, vol. 1 (Paris: Champion, 1998), 267–77.

L'orrez lur veint del orïent
Quis en meinet vers occident.
Tutes perdent les veüthes
Fors de la mer e des nües. [25]
Pur le bon vent ne se feignent,   215
Mais de nager mult se peinent,
E desirent pener lur cors
A ço vetheir pur quei vunt fors.
   Si cururent par quinze jurs,
Desque li venz tuz lur fud gurz;   220
Dunc s'esmaient tuit li frere
Pur le vent qui falit ere.
Li abes dunc les amonestet,
Qui curages unc ne cestet:
'Metez vus en Deu maneie,   225
E n'i ait nul qui s'esmaie.
Quant averez vent, siglez sulunc;
Cum venz n'i ert, nagez idunc.'
As aviruns dunc se metent,
La grace Deu mult regretent,   230
Quer ne sevent quel part aler,
Ne quels cordes dient haler,
Quel part beitrer, quel part tendre,
Ne u devrunt lur curs prendre.
Un meis sanz vent nagent tut plein   235
Tuit li frere par nul desdeign;

---

[25] For a discussion concerning the term 'nuage' see Burgess, 'Les fonctions des quatre éléments,' p. 14.

The Anglo-Norman Voyage of St Brendan

The breeze comes to them from the east
Which takes them towards the west.
They lose sight of everything
Apart from the sea and the clouds.
Although there is a favourable wind, they are not idle
But they toil very much with their rowing
And wish to tax the strength of their bodies
In order to see that for which they are leaving home.
    Thus they sailed for fifteen days,
Until all the winds became sluggish for them;
Then all the brothers were dismayed
On account of the wind which had ceased.
Then the abbot admonished them,
He whose courage never stumbled[26]
'Place yourselves under God's protection
And let there be no one who is dismayed.
When there is wind, sail in the same direction as it;
When there is no wind row accordingly.'
They therefore settle down to their oars,
They cry out loudly for God's favour,
For they do not know in which direction to go,
Nor which ropes they should haul,
In which direction to steer, nor which direction to aim for,
Nor where they should direct their course.
For a month they row entirely without wind
All the brothers without complaint;

---

[26] Burgess: 'Telling them *[the brethren]* not to lose heart.' Burgess uses Short and Merrilees who print *cesset*. Waters corrects this to *cestet*, 'stumbles.' Short and Merrilees point out that *qui* could be interpreted as *cui* 'whose', as I have used it here, or as a conjunction, as Burgess does. I am grateful to Glyn Burgess for his guidance on this matter.

Tant cum durat lur vitaile
Pener pourent sanz defaile.
Force perdent e viande;
Pur oc ourent poür grande. 240
     Cum lur avient granz busuinz,
A ses fetheilz Deus nen est luinz;
Pur oc ne deit hoem mescreire.
Cil ki enprent pur Deu eire
Tant en face cum faire pout; 245
Deus li truverat ke lui estout.
Terre veient grande e halte;
Li venz lur vient san defalte.
Qui de nager erent penét
Sanz tuz travalz la sunt menét, 250
Mais n'i truvent nul' entrethe
U lur nef fust eschipede,
Quer de rocheiz ert aclose
U nul d'eals tuz munter n'ose.
Halt sunt li pui, en l'air tendant, 255
E sur la mer en luin pendant.
Des creos desuz la mer resort,
Pur quei peril i at mult fort.
Amunt, aval port i quistrent,
E al querre treis jurs mistrent. 260
Un port truvent, le se sunt mis,
Qui fud trenched al liois bis,
Mais n'i out leu fors de une nef;
Cil fud faitiz el rocheit blef.

The Anglo-Norman Voyage of St Brendan

For as long as their victuals lasted
They could exert themselves without respite.
They lose their strength and food;
On this account they had great fear.

    When a great need befalls them,
God is not far from his faithful servants;
Of this no man should doubt.
He who undertakes a journey for God
Should do as much as he is able;
God will find him what he needs.
They see a land big and high;
The wind blows for them without stopping.
Those for whom rowing had become a toil
Are taken there without any hardship,
But they find no entrance
Where their ship could be moored,
For it was surrounded completely by rocks
Where not one of them dared ascend.
The hills are high stretching into the sky
And suspended far above the sea.
From the hollows beneath, the sea eddies back
Because of which there is very great danger.
Upwards and downwards they looked for a harbour
And they spent three days in their search.
They find a harbour, they have landed there,
Which was cut in the grey limestone
But there was room only for one ship;
This [harbour] was made in the pale rock.

Ferment la nef, eisent s'en tuit, 265
Vunt la veie qui bien les duit;
Dreit les meinet a un castel
Qui riches ert e grant e bel,
E resemblout mult regal leu,
D'empereür mult riche feu. 270
Entrerent enz dedenz le mur
Qui tuz ert faiz de cristal dur;
Paleiz veient tuz a marbre,
N'i out maisun faite de arbre;
Gemmes od l'or funt grant clartét 275
Dun entailét sunt li parét;
Mais une rien mult lur desplout,
Que en la citét hume n'i out.
Dunc esguardent l'alçur palais,
Entrent enez el nun de pais. 280
    Enz el palais Brandan s'est mis,
E sur un banc puis s'est asis.
Fors sul les soens altres n'i vit;
Prent a parler, si lur ad dit:
'Alez querre par cez mesters 285
Si rien i at dun est mesters.'
Alerent cil e truverent
Ço que plus dunc desirerent,
Ço fud sucurs de viande,
E de beivre plentét grande,[27] 290

---

[27] The uses of 'drinking water' are discussed in Burgess, 'Les fonctions des quatre éléments,' p. 11.

The Anglo-Norman Voyage of St Brendan

The Uninhabited City

They make fast the ship, they all disembark,
They follow the road that leads them clearly;
It led them straight to a castle
Which was rich and big and beautiful,
And seemed like a very royal place,
The estate of a very rich emperor.
They went in inside the walls
Which were all made of hard crystal;
They see a palace all in marble,
There were no houses made of wood;
Gems with gold make great brightness
With which the walls are decorated;[28]
But one thing displeased them greatly,
That there was no man within the city.
Thus they gaze at the lofty palace,
And enter therein in the name of peace.

    Brendan has gone into the palace,
And then has sat down on a bench.
He did not see anyone else other than his men;
He begins to speak and has said to them:
'Go and look in these kitchen larders
If there is anything of which we have need.'
They went there and found
That which they then most desired,
This was a supply of food,
And a great abundance of drink

---

[28] Compare this with the description of the New Jerusalem in Revelation 21.

De or e de argent la vaisele
Que forment fud bone e bele.
Quanque voldrent tut a plentét
Trovent iloec u sunt entrét.
L'abes lur dist: 'Portez nus ent. 295
N'en prengez trop, ço vus defent.
E prïez Deu chescun pur sei
Que ne mentet vers Deu sa fai.'
Pur ço les volt li abes guarnir,
Quer bien purvit que ert a venir. 300
Cil aportent asez cunrei,
E n'en prestrent a nul desrei;
Tant mangerent cume lur plout,
E cum idunc lur en estout.
De Deu loër ne se ublïent, 305
Mais sa merci mult la crïent.

Del herberger pregnent oser;
Quant fud l'ure, vunt reposer.
Cum endormit furent trestuit,
Ast vos Sathan qui l'un seduit:[29] 310
Mist l'en talent prendre an emblét
Del or qu'il vit ensemblét.
L'abes veilout, e bien vetheit
Cum diables celui teneit,
Cum lui tendeit un hanap de or– 315
Plus riche n'at en nul tresor.

---

[29] 'infantem scilicet ethiopem,' Selmer, *Nauigatio*, *caput* VI, l. 56.

The Anglo-Norman Voyage of St Brendan

The crockery was of gold and silver
Which was very good and fine.
Whatsoever they had wished for, all in abundance
They found there in that place where they have entered.
The abbot said to them: 'Bring us some.
Do not take too much, this I forbid you
And pray to God each one for himself
That you do not break your faith with God.'
Because the abbot wished to warn them
For he well foresaw what was to come.
They brought sufficient provisions,
And they did not take any excess of it;
They ate as much as pleased them,
And as much as they then needed.
They did not forget to pray to God,
But they call out greatly for his mercy there.

The Stolen Goblet

They venture to stay for the night;
When it was time they go to rest.
When they had all gone to sleep,
Behold Satan who seduces one of them:
He made him desirous to take by stealth
Gold which he saw collected there.
The abbot was awake and saw well
How the devil had a hold on him,
And how he held out to him a golden goblet –
There is nothing richer in any treasury.

Cil levet sus, prendre l'alat,
E en repost tost l'enmalat;
E puis que out fait le larecin,
Revint dormir en sun reclin.   320
Tut vit l'abes u reposout,
Cum cil freres par nuit errout;
Pur tenebres ne remaneit:
Sanz candeile tut le vetheit,
Quar quant ço Deus li volt mustrer,   325
Sur ço ne stout cirge alumer.

    Treis jurs enters sujurnerent,
E puis al quart s'en turnerent.
Brandans lur dist: 'Seignurs, vus pri,
N'en portez rien od vus d'ici,   330
Neïs un punt de cest cunrei,
N'enteins l'aigue pur nule sei.'
Forment plurant dist as freres:
'Veiez, seignurs, cist est leres.'
Cil s'aparceut que l'abes sout   335
Del larecin; cument il l'out
Cunuit; a tuz confés se rent,
As pez le abét mercit atent.
Dist lur abes: 'Prïez pur lui,
Vus le verrez murrir encui.'   340
Devant trestuz tuz veables
Eisit criant li diables:
'Cheles, Brandan, par quel raisun
Gettes mei fors de ma maisun?'
Dist al frere ço que il volt,   345
Mercit li fait, e puis l'asolt.

The Anglo-Norman Voyage of St Brendan

The monk got up, went to take it,
And quickly stowed it away secretly;
And then when he had committed the theft,
Came back to sleep in his resting-place.
The abbot saw all from where he was resting,
As this brother wandered around by night;
On account of the darkness he did not fail
Without a candle: he saw it all,
For when God wanted to show him this
He did not need to light a taper.

They stayed for three full days
And then on the fourth they went away.
Brendan said to them: ' Gentlemen, I pray you,
Do not take anything away with you from here;
Even the smallest amount of these provisions,
Not even water for any thirst.'[30]
Weeping greatly he said to the brethren:
'Behold, gentlemen, this man is a thief.'
The latter understood that the abbot knew
About the theft; and how he had
Found out about it; he makes his confession to all,
At the abbot's feet he waits for mercy.
The abbot said to them: 'Pray for him
You will see him die today.'
Before everyone of them, visible to all,
The devil comes out, shouting:
'Come now, Brendan, for what reason
Are you throwing me out of my house?'
He said what he wanted to the brother,
He pardons him, and then absolves him.

---

[30] Cf. Stokes, 'Máel Dúin,' pp. 476–79.

Des que receut cumungement,
Veanz trestuz la mort le prent;
Le spirit en vait en paraïs,
En grant repos u Deus l'at mis.   350
Al cors firent sepulture,
Prïent Deu qu'en prenget cure.
Icist fud un des tres freres
Qu'en la nef receut li peres.

Vindrent al port el rivage;   355
Ast vus mult tost un message:
Pain lur portet e le beivre,
E sis rovet cel receivre.
Puis lur ad dit: 'Soür seez,
Quelque peril que vus veiez;   360
Que que veiez, n'aëz poür:
Deus vus durat mult bon oür,
E ço verrez que alez querant,
Par la vertud de Deu la grant.
E de cunrei nen esmaëz   365
Que vus ici asez n'aiez:
Ne frat faile desque vendrez
En icel liu u plus prendrez.'
Parfunt clinant, saisit les en;
Plus ne lur dist, meis alat s'en.   370

As soon as he received communion,
In the sight of all death takes him;
The spirit goes to Paradise,
In complete rest where God has placed him.
They buried the body,
And pray to God that he take care of it.
This was one of the three brothers
Which the father received on to the ship.

God provides all necessities

They came to the haven and the shore
Behold very soon a messenger:
He brings them bread and drink,
And he asks them to accept it.[31]
Then he has said to them: 'Be sure,
Whatever danger you see,
Whatever you see, do not be afraid:
God will give you very good fortune,
And you will see that which you are going looking for
By the great grace of God.
And do not be concerned about provisions
And the fact that you do not have enough here:
They will not be lacking until you come back
To this place where you will take more.'
Bowing deeply, he handed [bread and drink] over to them;
He did not say any more, but went away.

---

[31] Cf. Jesus feeding the five thousand in Matthew 14:15–21; Mark 6: 30–44; Luke 9: 11–17; 6: 1–14.

Or unt voüt li Deu servant
Que il eirent par Deu cumant,
E unt pruvét tut a soüt
Par miracles que unt voüt;
E bien veient que Deus les paist. 375
De loër Deu nuls ne se taist.

Siglent al vent, vunt s'en adés,
Li cunduz Deu mult lor est pres.
Curent par mer grant part del an,
E merveilles trestrent ahan. 380
Terre veient a lur espeir,
Cum de plus luin lur pout pareir
Drechent lur nef icele part,
E n'i at nul del nager tart.
Lascent cordes, metent veil jus, 385
Ariverent e sailent sus.
Veient berbiz a grant fuisun,
A chescune blanches tuisun;
Tutes erent itant grandes
Cun sunt li cerf par ces landes. 390
Dist lur l'abes: 'Seignures, d'ici
Ne nus muverum devant terz di.
Jusdi est oi de la ceine,[32]
Cum li filz Deu suffrit peine.

---

[32] Cf. ll. 831 and 881. There 'la ceine' (The Last Supper) is referred to as 'lur mandét'.

The Anglo-Norman Voyage of St Brendan

Now God's servants have seen
That they are travelling by God's command,
And this has been proved to each one beyond doubt
By virtue of the miracles that they have seen;
And they see that God is feeding them.
In praising God no one is silent.

The Isle of Sheep

They sail in the wind, and go away forthwith,
The protection of God is very close to them.
They sail on the sea for the best part of the year,
And endure extreme hardship.
They see land in accordance with their hope
As far off as it could be visible to them.[33]
They turn their ship in this direction,
And none of them are slow to row there.
They slacken the ropes, take the sail down,
They came to land and jump ashore.
They see sheep in great abundance,
Each with a white fleece;
Every one was as large
As stags are in these woodlands.
The abbot said to them: 'Gentlemen, from here
We shall not move before the third day.
Today is Maundy Thursday,
When the Son of God suffered torment.

---

[33] Burgess: 'on the distant horizon.'

Il nus est douz e prest amis, 395
Qui prestement nus as tramis
Dunt poüm sa feste faire.
Pensez de la nef sus traire.
De icez berbiz une pernez,
Al di pascal la cunreez; 400
A Deu cungét de ço ruvum,
Altre quant nus or n'i truvum.'
Que cumandat, iço fait unt,
E par tres dis ileoc estunt.
Al samadi lur vient uns mes, 405
De la part Deu salüet les.
Peil out chanut, oilz juvenilz;
Mult out vescut sanz tuz perilz.
Pain lur portet de sun païs[34]
Granz e mult blanz guasteus alis; 410
E si lur falt neüle rein,
Tut lur truverat, ço promet bien.
L'estre d'iloc l'abes anquist;
Ne sai s'osat, mais poi l'en dist.
Ço respundit: Asez avum 415
Quanque des quers penser savum.'
E dist l'abes, 'berbiz ad ci,'
Unc en nul leu tant grant ne vi.'

---

[34] Cf. l. 141. If Short and Merrilees are correct in their assertion that the messenger is also the angel who guides the brethren on their journey (ll. 140–41), then the bread would represent manna from heaven (Exodus 16:15).

The Anglo-Norman Voyage of St Brendan

He is a kind and present friend to us,
Who has readily sent us
That with which we can celebrate his feast.
Think to drag the boat ashore.
Take one of these sheep,
Prepare it for Easter Day;
We shall ask God's permission for this
Seeing that we cannot find anyone else.'
They have done what he commanded
And for three days they remain there.
On the Saturday a messenger comes to them,[35]
He greets them on God's behalf.
He had hoary hair, youthful eyes;
He had lived long without any danger.
He brought them bread from his country:
Big and very white unleavened loaves[36]
And if they are short of anything,
He will find everything for them, this he promises faithfully.
The abbot inquired about the nature of that place;
I don't know how helpful he was, but he did say a little about it.[37]
The other replied: 'We have in abundance
Whatever our hearts are able to imagine.'
And the abbot said, 'There are sheep here,
Bigger than I ever saw anywhere.'[38]

---

[35] Burgess: 'Sunday'. Waters and Short and Merrilees have this as 'Saturday'.
[36] These loaves would have been of wheaten flour.
[37] The translation of this line is problematic: here I follow Burgess's translation. 'Oser' translates as 'to dare' or 'to be so bold'. Short and Merrilees (p. 84) translate this as 'I do not know if he was forthcoming (?), bur he told him little about it'
[38] Cf. Orchard, *Pride and Prodigies*, p. 184.

Respunt lui cil: 'N'est merveille:
Ja ci traite n'ert öeile;   420
L'ivers nen i fait rancune,
Ne d'enfertét n'i mort une.
A cel' isle que tu veis la,
Entre en ta nef, Brandan, e va.
En cel' isle anuit estras   425
E ta feste demain i fras.
Demain enz nuit en turnerez;
Per quei si tost, bien le verrez.
Puis revendrez, e sanz peril,
Bien pres siglant de cest costil;   430
E puis irez en altre liu,
U jo en vois e la vus siu,
Mult pres d'ici; la vus truverai,
Asez cunrei vus porterai.'

Siglet Brandan, nel cuntredit,   435
Vail al isle que il bien vit.
Vent out portant e tost i fud,
Mais bein grant mer out trescurud;
E issi vait qui Deus maine.
Terre prennent, e sanz peine;   440
Eissent s'en fors tuit li frere
Fors sul l'abes qui enz ere.
Beal servise e mult entrin
Firent la nuit e le matin.

The Anglo-Norman Voyage of St Brendan

The other replies to him: 'It is no marvel:
The sheep here are never milked;
The winter is not inclement,
Nor did any one of them die of sickness here.
Board your ship, Brendan, and go)
To that island which you see there.)
Tonight you will stay on that island
And you will celebrate your feast there tomorrow.
Tomorrow before nightfall you will leave it;
You will see clearly why so soon.
Then you will come back, and without danger,
Sailing quite close to this coast;
And then you will go to another place,
Where I am departing for and following you there,
Very close to here: I will find you there,
I will bring you enough provisions.'

The Great Fish

Brendan sails, he doesn't contradict him,
He goes to the island which he saw clearly.
He had a favourable wind and he was soon there,
But he had sailed across a very large stretch of sea;
This is how things turn for those whom God guides.
They land ashore, and without difficulty;
All the brothers disembark
Except for the abbot alone who stayed on board.
They had fine and very sincere divine services
At night and in the morning.

Puis que unt tut fait lur service 445
En la nef cum en iglise,
Charn de la nef, qu'il i mistrent,
Pur quire la dunc la pristrent;
De la busche en vunt quere,[39]
Dunt le manger funt a terre. 450
Cum li mangers fud cunreez,
Dist li bailis: 'Or aseez.'
Dunc s'escrïent mult haltement:
'A! donz abes, quar nus atent!'
Quar la terre tute muveit, 455
E de la nef mult s'en fuieit.
Dist li abes: 'Ne vus tamez,
Mais Damnedue mult reclamez;
E pernez tut nostre cunrei,
Enz en la nef venez a mei.' 460
Jetet lur fuz e bein luncs raps.
Parmi tut ço muilent lur dras.
Enz en la nef entré sunt tuit;
Mais lur isle mult tost s'en fuit:
De dis liwes bien choisirent 465
Le fou sur lui qu'il i firent.
Brandan lur dist: 'Freres, savez
Pur quei poür oüt avez?
N'est past terre, ainz est beste
U feïmes notre feste, 470

---

[39] For a discussion of 'feu' see Burgess, 'Les fonctions des quatre éléments,' pp. 16–20

The Anglo-Norman Voyage of St Brendan

After they have all completed their service
In the ship as if in church,
Meat from the ship that they [had] put there,
They took out to cook there;
They go off to look for firewood,
With which to make their meals on land.
When the meal was prepared,
The steward said: 'Now sit down.'
Then they cry out very loudly:
'Ah! Lord abbot, wait for us!'
For the whole earth was moving,
And moving far away from the ship.
The abbot said: 'Do not be afraid,
But pray fervently to the Lord God;
And take all our provisions,
And come to me on board the ship.'
He threw them poles and very long ropes[40]
During all this they wet their clothes.
They all boarded the ship;
But their island rapidly moved away
From ten leagues away they saw clearly
The fire on it that they [had] made there.
Brendan said to them: 'Brothers, do you know
Why you have been afraid?
It is not land, but a beast
Where we performed our feast,

---

[40] 'Raps' – (ropes), an English loanword used by Benedeit which Short, amongst others, suggest demonstrates that the Anglo-Norman *Voyage* was composed in England, see Ian Short, '*Tam Angli Quam Franci*: Self-definition in Anglo-Norman England,' *Anglo-Norman Studies* 18 (1995): 153–75, p. 155. Other loanwords used by Benedeit include *hasps* (l. 688) and *baz/bat* (boat, ll. 602, 890).

Pessuns de mer sur les greinurs.
Ne merveillés de ço, seignurs.
Pur ço vus volt Deus ci mener
Que il vus voleit plus asener.
Ses merveilles cum plus verrez, 475
En lui mult mielz puis encrerrez:
Mielz le crerrez e plus crendrez,
A sun comant plus vus prendrez.
Primes le fist li reis divins
Devant trestuz pessuns marins. 480

Quant out ço dit l'abes Brandan,
Bien ad curut de mer grant pan.
Vient terre halte e clere,
Si cum lur out dit cil frere.
Venent i tost e arivent, 485
Ne del eisir ne s'eschivent,
Ne pur altre rein ne dutent,
Mais a terre la nef butent;
Amunt un duit s'en vunt süef,
E od cordes traient lur nef. 490
Al chef del duit out une arbre

A sea fish greater than the greatest.[41]
Do not be astonished by that, gentlemen.
God wanted to lead you here for this
Because He wanted to instruct you.
The more you will see His wonders,
The better by far you will then believe in Him;
The better you will trust Him and the more you will fear him,
The more you will obey his command.
First in rank the divine king made
This sea fish above all others.[42]

The Paradise Of Birds[43]

After the abbot Brendan had said this,
He sailed a great distance of sea.
They see land high and clear,
Just as that brother had told them.
They soon arrive there and come to land,
Nor do they shun the landing,
Nor do they fear anything else,
But push the ship ashore;
They go off gently up a stream,
And drag their ship with ropes.
At the upper end of the stream was a tree

---

[41] Plummer, Lives of the Irish Saints, I, pp. 97–98, also Edward William Lane, *The Thousand and One Nights*, 3 vols., (London: Charles Knight and Co., 1841), vol. 3, p. 7.
[42] Cf. Genesis 1: 21.
[43] Cf. Stokes, 'Máel Dúin,' pp. 492–93; Stokes, 'Húi Corra,' pp. 42–43 and 48–49; Stokes, 'Snedgus,' pp. 20–21.

Itant blanche cume marbre,
E les fuiles mult sunt ledes,
De ruge e blanc taceledes.
De haltece par vedue   495
Muntout l'arbre sur la nue;
Des le sumét desque en terre
La brancheie mult la serre
E ledement s'estent par l'air,
Umbraiet luin e tolt l'escair,   500
Tute asise de blanc oiseus–
Unches nuls hom ne vit tant beus.
Li abes prent a merveiller,
E prïet Deu sun conseller
Que li mustret quel cose seit,   505
Si grant plentét d'oiseus que deit,
Quel leu ço seit u est venuz,
D'içò l'asent par ses vertuz.
Sa prïere quant la laisat,
L'un des oiseus s'en devalat;   510
Tant dulcement sonat li vols
En eschele cum fait li cols;
E puis qu'asist desur la nef,
Brandan parlat bel e süef:
'Si tu es Deu criature,   515
De mes diz dunc prenges cure.
Primes me di que tu seies,
E en cest liu que tu deies,
E tu e tuit cil altre oisel,
Pur ço que me semblez mult bel.'   520
L'oiseil respunt: 'Angele sumes,

The Anglo-Norman Voyage of St Brendan

As white as marble
And the leaves are very broad,
Spotted with red and white.
Judging the height by the eye
The tree rose up above the cloud;
From the summit to the ground
The branches surround it very closely
And extend widely through the air,
It casts shade a long way and takes away the light,
It is all occupied by white birds –
Never did one see any so beautiful.
   The abbot begins to marvel,
And prays to God his counsellor
That He should explain to him the cause
And meaning of such an abundance of birds,
What place this is where he has come,
And that with his powers He should instruct him about this.
When he ended his prayer,
One of the birds flew down;
The flight sounded so sweetly
Like the stroke of a bell does;
And after it sat down on the ship,
Brendan spoke finely and gently:
'If you are God's creature,
Then pay heed to my words.
First tell me who you are,
And what your duties are in this place,
Both your own and [those of] these other birds,
Because you seem very fine to me.'
The bird replies: 'We are angels,

E enz en ceil jadis fumes;
E chaïmes de halt si bas
Od l'orguillus e od le las
Par superbe qui revelat, 525
Vers sun seignur mal s'eslevat.
Cil fut sur nus mis a meistre,
De vertuz Deu nus doust paistre;
Pur oc que fut de grant saveir,
Sil nus estout a meistre aveir. 530
Cil fud mult fels par superbe,
En desdein prist la Deu verbe.
Puis que out ço fait, lui servimes,
E cum anceis obedimes;
Pur ço sumes deseritét 535
De cel regne de veritét.
Mais quant iço par nus ne fud,
Tant en avum par Deu vertud:
N'avum peine se cume cil
Qui menerent orguil cum il. 540
Mal nen avum fors sul itant:
La majested sumes perdant,
La presence de la glorie,
E devant Deu la baldorie.
Le num del leu que tu quesis, 545
C'est as Oiseus li Paraïs.'
E il lur dist: 'Or ad un an
Que avez suffert de mer le han;
Arere sunt uncore sis
Anz que vengez en paraïs. 550

The Anglo-Norman Voyage of St Brendan

And formerly we were in heaven;
And we fell from on high so low
With the proud and the wretched one
Who through pride rebelled,
Rose treacherously against his lord.[44]
He was placed as master over us,
He was duty-bound to feed us with God's virtues;
Because he had great knowledge,
It was necessary for us to accept a master.
That one was most disloyal through pride,
He scorned the word of God.
After he had done this we served him,
And as before we obeyed him;
Because of this we have been disinherited
From that kingdom of truth.
But since this was not caused by us,
We have all this by God's power:
We do not share the same punishment as those
Who showed pride like him.
We have no suffering except only this:
We are deprived of majesty,
The presence of glory,
And joy before God.
The name of the place that you asked about,
It is the Paradise of Birds.'
And he [the bird] said to them: 'Now it has been a year
That you have suffered the fatigue of the sea;
There are another six
Years before you come to Paradise.

---

[44] Revelation 12: 7–9; cf. Dante, *Inferno*, canto III.

Mult suffereiz peines e mal
Par occean, amunt, aval,
E chescun an frez la feste
De la Pasche sur la beste.'
Puis que out ço dit, si s'en alat 555
Ensum l'arbre dunm devalat.
    Quant vint del jurn al declinant,
Vers le vespre dunc funt un cant;
Od dulces voiz mult halt crïent
E enz el cant Deu mercïent 560
C'or unt veüd en lur eisil
Itel cumfort cum erent cil.
Humaine gent unches anceis
N'i enveiat li suvereins reis.
Dunc dist l'abes: 'Avez oïd 565
Cum cist angele nus unt goïd?
Loëz en Deu e gracïez:
Plus vus aimet que ne quïez.'
La nef leisent en l'aiguage,
E mangerent al rivage; 570
E puis chantent la cumplie
Halt od mult grant psalmodie.
Puis enz as liz tuit se spandent
E a Jesu se cumandent.
Dorment cum cil qui sunt lassét 575
E tanz perilz qui unt passét;
Mais nepurtant a chant de gals
Matines dïent ainz jurnals,
E as refreiz ensemble od eals
Respunt li cors de cez oiseals. 580

The Anglo-Norman Voyage of St Brendan

You will suffer much hardship and trouble
On the ocean, upwards and downwards,
And every year you will celebrate the feast
Of Easter upon the beast.'
After he had said this, he went away
To the top of the tree whence he descended.

   When the day was drawing to an end,
Towards evening accordingly they sing a hymn;
They cry out very loudly with sweet voices,
And in the hymn they thank God
For they have seen in their exile
Comfort such as they have.
The supreme king never before   )
Sent members of the human race there.)
Accordingly the abbot said: 'Have you heard
How well these angels have welcomed us?
Praise God for this and give thanks:
He loves you more than you think.'
They leave the ship in the channel,
And eat on the shore;
And then they sing compline
Loudly with very great psalmody.
Then they all stretch out in their beds
And commend themselves to Jesus.
They sleep like ones who are wearied
And who have passed through so many dangers;
But nevertheless at the cock-crow
They say matins as on every day,
And to the refrain together with them
The chorus of birds responds.

En prime main al cler soleil
Ast vus venant le Deu fedeil
Par qui asen unt cest avei,
E par sun dun unt le cundrei.
Cil lur ad dit: 'De viande 585
Jo vus truverai plentét grande;
Asez averez, e sanz custe,
Desque uitaves Pentecuste.
Puis les travalz estout sujurn:
Dous meis estrez ici enturn.' 590
Dunc prent cungé e s'en alat,
E al terz di la repairat;
Dous feiz tuzdis la semaine
Cil revisdout la cumpaine.
Cum lur ad dit, eissil firent; 595
En sun enseign tut se mistrent.
 Quant vint li tens de lur errer,
Lur nef prengnent dunc a serrer;
De quirs de buf la purcusent,
Quar cil qu'i sunt plein usent; 600
Asez en unt a remüers
Que estre puisset lur baz enters.
E bein de tut se guarnissent,
Pur defalte ne perisent.
Cil lur liverat pain e beivre 605
Cum il voldrent plus receivre;
Tut ad cunté a pleins uit meis:

The Anglo-Norman Voyage of St Brendan

Preparations For The Second Year

At sunrise in the bright sunlight
Behold God's faithful messenger coming
By whose teaching they have this guidance,
And by whose gift they have their food and drink.
He has said to them: 'Of food
I will find for you great abundance;
You will have enough, and without trouble,
Until the Octave of Pentecost.[45]
After your hardships rest is necessary:
You will be here for about two months.'
Then he takes his leave and went away,
And on the third day he reappeared there;
Twice each week
He visited the company.
They did as he has told them;
They placed themselves under his complete guidance.
  When the time came for their departure
They begin accordingly to make their ship watertight;
They sew oxhides all over it,
For those which are on it are completely worn out;
They have enough of them and to spare,
So that their boat may be sound.
And they provide themselves well with everything,
So that they do not perish through want [of anything].
The [messenger] delivered bread and drink
As much as they needed;
He has calculated everything for fully eight months:

---

[45] The Sunday after Whitsun.

La nef ne pout plus suffrir peis.
Quant cil e cil baisét se sunt,
Prengent cungét e puis s'en vunt. 610
Cil lur mustrat od mult granz plurs
Quel part dourent tendre lur curs.
Ast vus l'oiseil desur le mast;
Dist a Brandan que s'en alast.
Grant curs li dist qu'ad a faire, 615
E mult ennois ad a traire;
Uit meis enters estreit baïs
Ainz que pusset entrer païs
Ainz qu'al isle vengent Albeu,
U estreient al Naël Deu. 620
Puis qu'out ço dit, plus ne targe;
Vait s'en al vent tost la barge.

Vunt s'en mult tost en mer siglant,
De tant bon vent Deu gracïant.
Crut lur li venz, e mult suvent, 625
Crement peril e grant turment.
Puis quatre meis veient terre,
Mais fort lur est a cunquerre;
E nepurtant a la parfin
Al siste meis virent la fin. 630
Prengent terre, mais nepuroec
Nul' entree truvent iloec;
Virun en vunt quarante dis,
Ainz que en nul port se seient mis,

The ship could not bear any more weight.
When the [messenger] and they have kissed,
They take their leave and then depart.
The [messenger] showed them with great weeping
In which direction they must set their course.
Behold the bird upon the mast;
He told Brendan that he had to leave.
He told him that he had a long voyage to do,
And many troubles to endure;
For eight full months they would be waiting expectantly
Before they could enter land,
Before they could come to the Isle of Ailbe,
Where they would be at Christmas.
When he had said this, he tarries no more;
The boat goes away quickly in the wind.

The Isle of Ailbe

They go sailing quickly away to sea,
Thanking God for such good wind.
The winds increased for them, and very often
They fear danger and great storm.
After four months they see land,
But it is very difficult for them to reach;
And nevertheless in the end
In the sixth month they saw the end.
They put in to land, but nevertheless
They do not find an entrance there;
Around they go for forty days,
Before they can enter any harbour,

Quar li rocheit e li munt grant 635
A la terre lur sunt devant.
Puis mult a tart truvent un cros
Que fait uns duiz, qui lur ad os.
Cil cundüent lur nef amunt;
Reposent sei, quar lassét sunt. 640
Puis dist l'abes: 'Eisum en fors,
Querums que seit mester as cors.'
Eisent s'en tuit e uns e uns,
L'abes ovoec ses cumpaignums,
E funtaine trovent duble, 645
L'une clere, l'altre truble.
Vunt i curant cum sedeillus.
Dist lur l'abes: 'Retenez vus.
Prendre si tost jol vus defent,
D'ici que avum parlé od gent. 650
Quel nature nus ne savum
Aient li duit trovez que avum.'
Les diz l'abét cil les crement,
E lur grand seif mult la prement.

    Hastivement, e nun a tart, 655
Ast vus currant un grant veilard.
Poür oussent, ne fust l'abit
Quar moines ert – mais rein ne dit.
Vient enchaër as pez Brandan;
Drechet lui sus cil par la main. 660

The Anglo-Norman Voyage of St Brendan

Because of the rocks and high mountains
Standing before them on the land.
Then very belatedly they find a hollow
Which a stream makes, which is of service to them.
They steer their ship upwards;
They take a rest, for they are tired.
Then the abbot says: 'Let's disembark,
Let's seek what is necessary for our bodies.'
They all disembark one by one,
The abbot with his companions,
And they find a double fountain
One clear, the other cloudy.[46]
They go running there as they are thirsty.
The abbot said to them: 'Restrain yourselves.
I forbid you to take anything so soon
From here until we have spoken with the people.
We do not know what is the nature of)
The watercourses that we have found.')
They [the companions] fear the words of the abbot,
And keep their great thirst well in check.

    Rapidly, and not long afterwards,
Behold a tall old man running.[47]
They would have been afraid, were it not for the habit –
For he was a monk – but he said nothing.
He comes and falls at Brendan's feet;
The latter raises the former up by the hand.

---

[46] The motif of two springs may derive from Plato's *Critias*, p. 1302; cf. Stokes, 'Húi Corra,' pp. 58–59.

[47] The Húi Corra also encounter a community of Ailbe's monks, see Stokes, 'Húi Corra,' pp. 56–57.

Clinet parfunt e humlement,
Le abét e tuz baiser enprent.
Puis prent Brandan par la destre
Pur mener l'en a sun estre;
As altres dist par sun signe 665
Vengent vedeir leu mult digne.
Cum alouent, l'abes ad quis
Quels leus ço seit u se sunt mis;
Mais cil se taist, respuns ne fait,
Goït les fort od mult duz hait. 670
Tant unt alét que ore veient
Le leu u il aler deient:
Abeïe bele e bone,
Plus sainte n'at suth le trone.
L'abes del leu fait porter fors 675
Ses reliques e ses tresors:
Cruz e fertres e les tistes
Bien engemmez de amestistes,
De or adubez e de peres
Preciuses e enteres, 680
Od encensers de or amassét
E les gemmes enz encassét
Li vestiment sunt tuit a or—
En Arabie nen at si sor
Od jagunces e sardines 685
Forment grandes e entrines;
Od tupazes e od jaspes
Itant cleres sunt les haspes.

The Anglo-Norman Voyage of St Brendan

He bows deeply and humbly,
He begins to embrace the abbot and all the others.
Then he takes Brendan by the right hand
To take him away to his place of abode;
He told the others by means of a sign
That they should come to see a most worthy place.
While they were going, the abbot has asked
What place this is where they have landed;
But the other is silent, makes no reply,
He welcomes them warmly with much kind joy.
They have gone so far that now they see
The place where they must go:
A good and fine abbey,
There is no holier one beneath the firmament,
The abbot of the place has its relics)
And treasures carried outside:)
Crosses and reliquaries and the ornamental metal covers
  for gospel-books
Richly studded with amethysts
Adorned with gold and with stones
Precious and whole,
With censers of solid gold,
And the gems set therein.
Their vestments are all of gold –
In Arabia there are none so reddish-golden
With jacinths and sards
Very big and perfect;
With topazes and jaspers
The clasps are just as bright.

Tuit li moine sunt revestud,
Od lur abét sunt fors eisud. 690
Od grant goie e grant dulceur
Processiun funt li seignur;
E quant baisét se sunt trestuit,
Chescun le altre par la main duit.
Meinent en lur abeïe 695
Brandan e sa cumpainie;
Servise funt bel e leger–
Nel voleient trop agreger.
Puis vunt manger en refraitur,
U tuit taisent fors li litur. 700
Devant eals unt dulz e blanc pain,
Bein savurét e forment sain;
Racines unt en lu de mes,
Qui sur deintz saülent les.
Puis unt beivre mult savurét 705
Aigue dulce plus de murét
Quant sunt refait, levét s'en sunt,
E versilant al muster vunt;
Vunt verseilant miserere
Desque en estals tuit li frere, 710
Fors sul iceals qui servirent:
En refreitur cil resirent.

    Quant l'eschele fud sonee,
Puis que l'ure fud chantee,
L'abes del leu fors les meinet; 715

The Anglo-Norman Voyage of St Brendan

All the monks are clothed in surplices,
[And] have come outside with their abbot.
With great joy and great kindness
The gentlemen make a procession;
And when everyone has embraced each other,
They lead each other by the hand.
They lead into their abbey
Brendan and his company;
They perform a beautiful and light divine service–
They did not wish to make it too heavy.
Then they go and eat in the refectory,
Where all are silent apart from the readers.[48]
Before them they have sweet and white bread,
Very sweet-tasting and very wholesome;
They have roots instead of a dish of prepared food,
Which satisfies them more than delicacies.
Then they have a very sweet-tasting drink:
Water sweeter than mulberry wine.
When they are refreshed, they have got up,
And go singing versicles in the monastery;
They go singing *miserere* versicles[49]
Until all the brothers reached the stalls,
Except alone for those who served:
They in their turn sat in the refectory.

    When the bell was rung,
[And] after the canonical hour was sung,
The abbot of the place led them outside;

---

[48] 1 Corinthians 14:25.
[49] Psalm 51; cf. Burgess, 'The Anglo-Norman Version,' p. 346, n. 9.

D'els e de lui lur enseignet,
Qui sunt, cument, des quant i sunt:
De qui, par qui succurs i unt:
'Nus sumes ci vint e quartre
Qui conversum en cest atre. 720
Uitante anz ad que prist sa fin
A saint Albeu le pelerin.
Riches hom fud, de mult grant fiu,
Mais tut guerpit pur icest leu.
Quant alat en tapinage, 725
Apparut lui Deu message;
Ça lamenat, trovat lui prest
Icest muster qu'uncore i est.
Quant oïmes en plusurs leus
Que ci maneit Albeus li pius, 730
Par Deu ci nus asemblames
Pur lui que nus mult amames.
Tant cum vesquit, lui servimes,
E cume abét obeïmes.
Puis que le ordre nus out apris, 735
E fermement nus out asis,
Dunc lui prist Deus de sei mult pres;
Uitante anz ad que prist decés.
Deus nus ad puis si sustenuz
Que nuls mals n'est sur nus venuz, 740
De nostre cors nul'enfertét,
Ne peisance ne amertét.
De Deu nus veint – el n'en savum –
La viande que nus avum;

The Anglo-Norman Voyage of St Brendan

He explained to them about themselves and himself,
Who they are, how, since when they are there,
From whom, and by whom they get food there:
'There are twenty-four of us here
Who dwell in this holy ground.
It is eighty years since died
Saint Ailbe the pilgrim.
He was a rich man, of very great estate,
But he abandoned everything for this place.
When he went into seclusion,
A messenger of God appeared to him;
He brought him, [where] he found ready for him
This monastery which is still there.
When we heard in several places
That the holy Ailbe dwelt here,
In God's name we assembled here
For the sake of him whom we loved.
For as long as he lived, we served him,
And obeyed him as our abbot.
After he had taught us the monastic rules,
And had got us firmly established,
Then God took him very close to himself;
It is eighty years since he died.
God has supported us so well since
That nothing bad has happened to us,
No sickness of our bodies,
Nor affliction nor hardship.
From God comes to us – we do not know anything else–[50]
The food that we have;[51]

---

[50] Burgess: 'We know of no other source'.
[51] Cf. 1 Kings 17:6.

Nus n'i avum nul loreür, 745
Ne n'i veduns aporteür,
Mais chescun jurn tut prest trovum,
Sanz ço qu'ailur nus nel ruvum,
Tute veie le jurn uvrer
Entre les dous un pain enter; 750
A di festal ai tut le men
Pur super, e chascun le son;
E des dous duiz que veïstes,
Dunt pur un poi ne preïstes,
Li clers est freiz, que al beivre avum, 755
Li trubles calz, dun nus lavum.
E as hures que nus devum
En noz lampes fou recevum,
Ne pur l'arsun que cist fous fait
Cire ne oile le plus n'en vait; 760
Par lui emprent, par lui esteint,
N'avum frere de ço se paint.
Ici vivum e sanz cure;
Nule vie n'avum dure.
Ainz que vostre venir sousum, 765
Volt Deus qu'a vus cunrei ousum;
Il le dublat plus que ne solt:
Bien sai que vus receivre volt.
Des Thephanie al uitme di
Dunc a primes muverez d'ici; 770
Desque dunches sujurnerez,
Puis a primes vus an irez.'

The Anglo-Norman Voyage of St Brendan

We have no servant here,
We do not see the one who brings it here,
But every day we find it quite ready,
Without us asking for it elsewhere,
Always on working days[52]
A whole loaf of bread between two;
On festive days I have one to myself
For supper, and everyone has his;
And of the two streams that you saw
From which you very nearly drew water
The clear one is cold, which we use for drink,
The cloudy one is hot, in which we wash.
And at the times when we need
We receive fire in our lamps,[53]
In spite of the burning that this fire does
Neither wax nor oil gets used up any more;
It lights and goes out on its own accord,
We have no brother who deals with that.
We live here and without any worries;
We do not have a hard life at all.
Before we knew about your visit
God wished that we had provisions for you;
He augmented it more than he was wont:
[So] I am well aware that he wants us to receive you.
On the last day of Epiphany
Then and no sooner you will depart from here;
Until then you will stay,
Then and no sooner you will go away.'

---

[52] Burgess: 'each week day'.
[53] Cf. Stokes, 'Máel Dúin,' pp. 476–79.

Dunc dist Brandans: 'N'est liu si chers
U mansisse si volunters.'
Respunt l'abes: 'Ço va quere 775
Pur quei moüs de ta terre;
Puis revendras en tun païs,
Ileoc muras u tu nasquis.
Muveras d'ici la semaine
As uitaves de Thephanie.' 780

Quant vint le jurn que l'abes mist,
Brandan de lui le cungé prist.
Li uns abes l'altre cunduit,
Ensemble od lui li moine tuit.
Entrent en mer, vent unt par Deu 785
Quis esluinet del isle Albeu.
Curent en mer par mult lunc tens,
Mais de terre unt nul asens.
Failent al vent e a cunreid,
Crut l'egre faim e l'ardant seid; 790
E la mer fud tant paisible
Pur quei le curs unt peinible:
Espesse fud cume palud;
Tel i out enz ne creit salud.
Deus les succurt par orage: 795
Terre veient e rivage,
E bien sevent li afamét
Que de Deu sunt forment amét.

The Anglo-Norman Voyage of St Brendan

Then Brendan said: 'There is no place so dear
Where I would remain so willingly.'
The abbot replies: 'Go and seek for that
For which you set out from your land;
Then you will return to your country,
There you will die where you were born.
You will depart from here in a week
Eight days after Epiphany.'

The Intoxicating Spring

When the day came which the abbot appointed,
Brendan took his leave of him.
The one abbot leads the other,
And together with him all the monks.
They set sail and thanks to God have a favourable wind
Which takes them away from the Isle of Ailbe.
They sail on the sea for a very long time,
But they have no indication of the direction of land.
They are without wind and provisions,
The bitter hunger and the burning thirst increased;
And the sea was so calm
That progress is difficult:
It was as dense as a marsh;[54]
Some of them on board have no belief in deliverance.
God comes to their aid with a storm:
They see land and a landing place,
And the hungry men know for sure
That they are greatly loved by God.

---

[54] Cf. Tierney, *Liber de mensura orbis terrae*, p. 74, ll. 31–32.

    Trovent tele lur entree
Cum se lur fust destinee.   800
Un duit unt cler e pessuns denz,
Si em pernent a plus que cenz.
Mester lur unt virun l'umeit
Herbes qui sunt el betumeit.
L'abes lur dist: 'N'aiez cure   805
De beivre trop sanz mesure.'
Cil em pristrent secund lur seid;
As diz abét ne tenent feid.
Tant em pristrent puis a celét
Pur quei furent fol apelét.   810
Quar li sumnes lur cureit sus
Dum il dormant giseient jus;
Qui trop beveit giseit enclins,
Tel jurn, tel dous, tel tres entrins.
Brandan priout pur ses muines,   815
Que il vedeit tuz suduines.
Des que en lur sens cil revindrent,
Pur fols forment tuit se tindrent.
Dist lur abes: 'Fuium d'ici,
Que ne chaiz meis en ubli.   820
Mielz vient suffrir honeste faim
Que ublïer Deu e sun reclaim.'

The Anglo-Norman Voyage of St Brendan

   They find their way in
As if it was pre-ordained.
They have a clear stream and fish therein,
And they catch more than a hundred of them there.
They have need of herbs which are   )
In the boggy ground around the riverbed.)
The abbot said to them: 'Do not desire
To drink too much immoderately.'
[The monks] drank from it according to their thirst;
They paid no heed to words of the abbot.
They took so much and afterwards in secret
On account of which they were called foolish.
For sleep fell upon them
So they lay down sleeping;
The ones who drank too much lay prostrate,
One for a day, another two, another three full days.
Brendan prayed for his monks
Whom he saw all flat out.[55]
As soon as [the monks] came back to their senses,
They all considered themselves very foolish.
The abbot said to them: 'Let us get out of here,
So that you are not forgetful again.
It is better to suffer honourable hunger
Than to forget God and his invocation.'

---

[55] Stokes, 'Máel Dúin (suite),' p. 71.

Par mer d'ileoc se sunt tolud,
Desque al jusdi vint absolud
Dunc reparat peres Brandan   825
En la terre u fud l'altre an.
Ast lur hoste, le veil chanud.
Al port lur ad un tref tendud;
Bained i ad les travailez,
E nuveals dras apareilez.   830
Funt la ceine e lur mandét,
Cum en escrit est cumandét,
E sunt ileoc desque al terz di.
Turnerent s'en al samadi,
E vunt siglant sur le peisun.   835
L'abes lur dist: 'Fors en eisum.'
Lur caldere qu'il perdirent
En l'an devant, or la virent;
Li Jacoines l'ad gwardee,[56]
Or l'unt sur lui retruvee;   840
Plus asoür sur lui estunt,
E lur feste plus bele i funt.
Tute la nuit desque al matin
De festïer ne firent fin;
Le di paschur celebrïent,   845
De lur hures ne s'ublïent.

---

[56] MS *A* is unique in preserving the name *Jacoines*. This is discussed by Burgess, 'The Use of Animals in Benedeit's Version', pp. 11–34.

The Anglo-Norman Voyage of St Brendan

Friends Revisited

They have departed from there by sea,
Until Maundy Thursday came;
Then father Brendan returned
To the land where he was the previous year.
Behold their host, the hoary old man.
At the harbour he has pitched a tent for them;
He has bathed the exhausted men,
And has made ready new clothes for them.
They perform the ceremony commemorative of the Last
    Supper and the Washing of Feet
As is required in scripture
And they are there until the third day.
They went away again on the Saturday,
And they go sailing on to the fish.
The abbot said to them: 'Let's disembark here.'
Their cauldron which they lost
The year before, now they saw;
Jasconius has kept it,
Now they have found it on him;
They are more secure on him
And they celebrate a most beautiful festival there.
All the night until the morning
They did not cease to celebrate the festival;
They celebrate Easter Day,
They do not forget their canonical hours.

Plus de midi ne targerent,
Mais dunc lur nef rechargerent;
Tut a leisir e tut süef
Entrent d'iloc enz en lur nef. 850
    Alat s'en tost e curt li sainz
Vers les oiseus u furent ainz;
Bein unt choisit l'abre blanche
E les oiseals sur la branche.
De luin en mer bien oïrent 855
Cum li oisel les goïrent;
De lur canter ne firent fin
Desque arivé sunt li marin.[57]
Traient lur nef amunt le gort
U l'an devant ourent lur port. 860
Ast lur hoste chi tent un tref;
Cunrei portet pleine sa nef.
Dist lur: 'Ci streiz del tens un poi.
A voz cungez jo m'en revoi.
Ici mandrez, e sanz custe, 865
Desque uitaves Pentecoste.
Ne dutez rein, ne demurai;
Quant mesters ert, vus succurrai.'
Ferment lur nef od chaeines,
E sunt ileoc uit semaines 870
Quant vint le tens de lur aler,
L'un des oiseals prent avaler;
Sun vol ad fait tut a cerne
Puis s'est asis sur la verne.

---

[57] Short and Merriless have 'li pelerin' where Waters has 'li marin'. Waters follows the metre.

The Anglo-Norman Voyage of St Brendan

They did not delay beyond mid-day,
But then they reloaded their ship;
All at leisure and all quietly
From there they board their ship.
    The saint soon went away and hurries
Towards the birds where they were before;
They have clearly picked out the white tree
And the birds on the branches.
From far out to sea they heard clearly
How the birds welcomed them;
They did not stop their singing
Until the sailors have arrived.
They drag their ship up the stream
Where the year before they had their haven.
Behold their host who is pitching a tent;
His ship was laden full of provisions
He said to them: 'You will be here a short time.
With your permission I am going back.
You will remain here, and without any hardship,
Until the octave of Pentecost.
Fear nothing, I shall not be a long time;
When it is necessary, I will come to your aid.'
They make their ship fast with chains,
And they are there eight weeks.[58]
When the time came for their departure,
One of the birds begins to fly down;
Its flight has made a big circle round,
Then it has alighted on the mast.

---

[58] Short and Merrilees have this as seven weeks.

Parler voldrat; Brandan le veit, 875
Dist a chescun que em pais seit.
'Seignurs', ço dist, 'a cest sujurn
Tuz cez set anz freiz vostre turn,
E chascun an al Naël Deu
Sujurnez en l'isle Albeu; 880
La ceine freiz e le mandét
U vostre hoste l'at cumandét;
E chescun an freiz la feste
De la Pasche sur la beste.'
Quant out ço dit, si s'en alat 885
Ensum l'arbre dum devalat.
La nef en mer parfunt flotet;
L'oste chescuns abootet,
Chi del venir ne s'est targét.
Vent de cunrei sun bat chargét, 890
E de sa nef charget la lur
Od bon cunrei de grant valur.
Puis apelet Filz Marie
Que guart cele cumpainie.
Del revenir metent termes 895
Al departir fundent lermes.

Trestout curent al portant vent
Chis fait errer vers occident.
Dormante mer unt e morte,
Chi a sigler lur est forte. 900
Puis q'unt curut tres quinzeines,

The Anglo-Norman Voyage of St Brendan

It will wish to speak; Brendan sees it,
He told everyone to be silent.
'Lords,' the former said, 'to this resting-place
You will make your return each of these seven years,
And every year at Christmas
You will stay on the Isle of Ailbe;
You will celebrate the Last Supper and the Washing of Feet
Where your host has commanded it;
And every year you will celebrate the feast
Of Easter on the beast.'
When it had said this, it went away
To the top of the tree from which it descended.
The ship floats deeply in the sea;
Everyone watches out for the host,
Who has not delayed his arrival.
He comes, his boat laden with provisions,
And from his vessel loads theirs
With good provisions of great value.
Then he calls upon the Son of Mary
That he may take care of this company.
They fix the appointed day for their return.
At the departure they shed tears.

The Fight of the Sea-Serpents

They sail with a completely favourable wind
Which makes them journey towards the west.
They have a sluggish and lifeless sea,
Which makes it difficult for them to sail.
When they have been under way for three fortnights,[59]

---

[59] 'Quinzeines,' literally 'three times fifteen days'.

Freidur lur curt par les veines,
Poür lur surt forment grande,
Que lur nef est tut en brande,
E poi en falt pur turmente 905
La nef od eals que n'adente.
Puis lur veint el dun s'esmaient
Plus que pur nul mal qu'il traient:
Vers eals veint uns marins serpenz,
Chis enchaced plus tost que venz. 910
Li fus de lui si enbraise
Cume buche de fornaise;
La flamme est grant, escalfed fort,
Pur quei icil crement la mort.
Sanz mesure grant ad le cors, 915
Plus halt braiet que quinze tors;
Peril n'i oust fors sul de denz,
Sil fuireient mil e cinc cenz.
Sul les undes que il muveit,
Pur grant turment plus ne stuveit. 920
Cum aprismout les pelerins,
Dun dist Brandan li veirs divins:
'Seignurs, n'entrez en dutance:
Deus vus en ferat la venjance.

The Anglo-Norman Voyage of St Brendan

Cold runs through their veins,
A great fear arises [in] them,
Because their ship is in great peril,
And it was very nearly the case because of a sudden swell
That the ship overturned with them in it.
Then something else came which dismayed them
More than any trouble that they endure:
Towards them came a sea serpent.
Which pursued them more quickly than the wind.
Its flames are fiery
Like the mouth of a furnace;[60]
The flame is great, it gives out great heat,
That is why they fear death.
Its body is great beyond measure,
It bellows more loudly than fifteen bulls;
Its teeth alone would have been a great threat to them,
One thousand and five hundred would have flown before it.[61]
Nothing more than the waves alone which it set in motion
Was necessary to make a great swell.[62]
As it approached the pilgrims,
Then Brendan, the true divine, said:
'Gentlemen, do not become frightened:
God will avenge you for it.
Guardez que pur fole poür   925

---

[60] Burgess: 'firewood'.
[61] ll. 917–18 are problematic. Waters has 'were there no peril save only for the teeth' (l. 917); Burgess has 'even if there have been fifteen hundred of them in the boat' (l. 918).
[62] Here I follow Waters's interpretation of the passage, but see Glyn S. Burgess, 'Repetition and Ambivalence in the *Anglo-Norman Voyage of St Brendan*,' *Anglo-Norman Anniversary Studies*, ed. Ian Short (London: Anglo-Norman Text Society, 1993): 61–74, p. 70.

Deu ne perdez ne bon oür;
Quar qui Deus prent en sun cunduit
Ne deit cremer beste qui muit.'
Puis que out ço dit a Deu urat;
Ço qu'out urét ne demurat.　　　　　　　　930
　　Altre beste veient venir,
Qui bien le deit cuntretenir.
Dreit cum ceste vers la nef traist,
L'altre qui vient a rage braist;
Ceste cunuit sa guarrere,　　　　　　　　　935
Guerpit la nef, traist s'arere.
Justedes sunt les dous bestes;
Drechent forment halt les testes;
Des narines li fous lur salt,
Desque as nües qui volet halt;　　　　　　940
Colps se dunent de lur noës,
Tels cum escuz, e des podes.
A denz mordanz se nafrerent,
Qui cum espez trenchant erent;
Salt en li sanz as aigres mors　　　　　　　945
Que funt li dent en cez granz cors;
Les plaies sunt mult parfundes,
Dun senglantes sunt les undes.
La bataile fud estulte,
En la mer out grant tumulte.　　　　　　　950
E puis venquit la dereine,
Morte rent la primereine;
A denz tant fort la detirat
Que en tres meitez la descirat;

The Anglo-Norman Voyage of St Brendan

Take care that for foolish fear
You do not lose God and good fortune;
For he who takes God for his protection
Must not fear any beast which roars.'
When he had said that, he prayed to God;
That for which he had prayed was not long delayed.

    They see another beast coming,
Which is to stand up to it well.
Like the first one it comes straight for the ship,
The second one which comes bellows furiously;
The first recognises its adversary,
Abandons the ship, and draws back.
The two beasts have [begun to] fight;
They raise their heads very high;
The fires gush from their nostrils,
And fly high up to the clouds;
They strike each other with their fins,
As with shields, and with their claws.
Biting with their teeth they wounded each other,
They were sharp like spears;
The blood gushes out from the fierce bites
Which the teeth make in these big bodies;
The wounds are very deep,
As a result of which the waves are bloody.
The battle was furious,
There was a great disturbance in the sea.
And then the second won the victory,
And kills the first one;
It pulled it about so much with its teeth
That it tore it up into three portions;

E puis que fist la venjance, 955
Realat a sa remanance.
Ne deit li hom mais desperer,
Ainz deit sa fait plus averer,
Quant veit que Deus si prestement
Vivere trovet e vestement, 960
E tanz succurs en perilz forz,
E estorses de tantes morz.
L'abes lur dist: 'Laisum tut el:
Signur servir bein deit l'um tel.'
Cil respunent mult volunters: 965
'Quar bien savum que nus as chers.'
Puis al demain terre vient,
E ariver bein se creient.

Vunt i mult tost e sailent fors
Pur reposer lur penez cors. 970
Sur l'erbeie tendent lur tref
E sus traient al secc lur nef.
Cum a terre ariverent,
Les tempestes aviverent;
Cunuit Brandans al air pluius 975
Que li tens ert mult annuus.
Li venz lur est cuntresailiz,
E li cunreiz lur est failiz;
Mais cil pur oc ne s'esmaient,
Quelque peril que il traient: 980

The Anglo-Norman Voyage of St Brendan

And when it had had its revenge,
It went back to its lair.
Man must not despair any more
But must establish more his faith as true,
When he sees that God so readily
Finds him food and clothing
And so much help in great peril,
And rescue from so many deaths.
The abbot said to them: 'Let's ignore everything else:
Man must serve such a lord.'
They reply very willingly:
'For we know very well that he holds us dear to him.'
Then on the following day they see land
And expect to come safely ashore.

The Voyagers Are Miraculously Fed

They go there very quickly and disembark
To rest their painful bodies.[63]
They pitch their tent on the greensward.
And drag their ship up on to the dry land.
As they landed ashore,
The storms got up again;
Brendan recognises from the rainy atmosphere
That the weather will be very troublesome.
The wind has risen up against them,
And their provisions are running out;
But they are not dismayed on this account:
No matter what peril they endure.

---

[63] Short and Merrilees has 'lassez' – 'weary' instead of 'penez' – 'painful'.

L'abes lur ad tant sermunét,
E Deus par tut asez dunét,
Que ne poient puint mescreire
De nule rien en lur eire.
Puis aprés ço, nïent a tart 985
Del peisun veint la terce part;
L'unde de mer tant la serre
Que ariver lur fait a terre;
La turmente sus la chacet,
Pur ço que a cez aise facet. 990
Dunc dist Brandans: 'Veiez, frere,
Ki enemis ainz vos ere
Or nus succurt par Deu grace;
Mangerez en grant espace.
Ne dutez rein, il nus ert past, 995
Quelque semblant qu'il nus mustrast;
Tant en pernez, as voz suspeis,
Que ne failet devant tres meis.'
Al sun cumant cil le firent:
A tant de tens se guarnirent. 1000
D'eigue dulce des funtaines
Funt lur tunes tutes pleines,
E de busche se guarnissent.
Puis q'unt l'uré, si s'en issent.

The Anglo-Norman Voyage of St Brendan

The abbot has preached to them so much,
And everywhere God has always given enough,
That they cannot doubt at all
About any single thing on their journey.
Then after this, not long afterwards,
The third portion of the fish comes;
The waves of the sea drives it onwards so much
That it makes it land ashore;
The sudden storm has driven it ashore,
In order that it might provide them with relief.
Then Brendan said: 'See, brothers,
That which was previously your enemy
Now helps us by the grace of God;
You will eat for a long while.
Fear nothing, there will be food for us,
However it may look to us;
Take as much of it, as you judge necessary,
So that it is not lacking within three months.'
They acted according to his command:
For so much time they stocked up.
Of soft water from the springs
They fill their barrels quite full,
And stock up with firewood.
Then when they have the breeze, they go away.

De miracles Deus ne cesset. 1005
Altre peril le apresset.
Si fust primers, ne fust meindres
Icist perilz, enz fust graindres;
Mais ne crement pur le purpens,
Qu'il unt de Deu, e le defens. 1010
Uns grips flammanz del air descent,
Pur eals prendre les ungles tent,
E flammantes ad les goës,
E trenchantes fort les poës.
Bord de la nef n'i ad si fort 1015
Sul od l'ungle que nel en port;
Pur sul l'aïr e le sun vent
Pur poi la nef achant ne prent.
Cum les caçout eisi par mer,
Vint uns draguns flammanz mult cler; 1020
Mot les eles e tent le col,
Vers le gripun drechet sun vol.
La bataile sus est en l'air;
Li fus d'els dous fait grant esclair;
Colps e flammes e mors e buz 1025
Se entredunent veiant eals tuz.
Li grips est granz, draguns maigres;
Cil est plus forz, cist plus aigres.
Morz est li grips, en mer chïat
Vengét en sunt kil unt haït. 1030
Vait s'en draguns od victorie;
Cil en rendent Deu la glorie.
Vunt s'en icil d'iloec avant;
Par le spirit Deu bein sunt savant.

The Anglo-Norman Voyage of St Brendan

Griffin versus Dragon

God does not cease to work miracles.
Another danger besets them.
If it had been the first of the two, this peril would not)
[in their estimation] have been smaller than the other, but)
   would have been greater;)
But they are not afraid on account of the regard
That they have for God, and his protection.
A flaming griffin comes down out of the air,
It stretches out its talons to take them,
And it has flaming cheeks,
And extremely sharp claws.
No plank of the ship would be strong enough
To prevent it from carrying it away with its claw;
Due to the mere force of its flight and the wind that it makes
The ship very nearly capsizes.
As it drove them thus over the sea,
A dragon came flaming very brightly;
It sets its wings in motion and stretches its neck,
And directs its flight towards the griffin.
The battle takes place up in the air;
The fires from both of them make a great light;
Blows and flames and bites and thrusts
They give each other with [the monks] all watching.
The griffin is big, the dragon lean;
The former is stronger, the latter fiercer.
The griffin is dead, it fell in the sea
Those who have hated it are avenged.
The dragon goes away with the victory
The former [i.e. the monks] give thanks to God.
They go forward away from there;
Through God's spirit they are very wise.

Vint la feste de saint Perrunt,   1035
Ki fud ocis el pred Nerunt;
Feste li funt cil e glorie,
A saint Perrunt l'apostorie.
Cum l'abes fist le servise,
Si cum la lei est asise,   1040
Chantout mult halt, a voiz clere.
Dunc li dïent tuit li frere:
'Beal pere chers, chante plus bas,
U si ço nun, perir nus fras
Quar tant cler' est chascun' unde,   1045
U la mer est plus parfunde,
Que nus veüm desque en terre,
E de peissuns tante guerre.
Peissun veüm granz e crüels –
Unc n'oïmes parler de tels.   1050
Si la noise les en commout,
Sachez murir que nus estout.'
L'abes surrist, e sis blasmat,
E pur mult fols les aasmat:
'Seignurs, de rein pur quei dutez?   1055
Voz creances cum debutez!
Perilz avez suffert plus granz,
Vers tuz fud Deus bons guaranz.
Uncore ore ne vus vint cist.
Clamez culpe!' Brandans lur dist.   1060
Chantat plus halt e forment cler.
Sailent bestes ruistes de mer,

The Anglo-Norman Voyage of St Brendan

The Congregation of Sea Monsters

The feast of St Peter the Apostle came
He who was killed in the gardens of Nero;
The former [i.e. the monks] celebrate his feast and glory,
To Saint Peter the first pope.
As the abbot performed the divine service,
And as the law prescribes,
He sang very loudly with a resonant voice.
Then all the brothers say to him:
'Wonderful dear father, sing more quietly,
Or if you do not you will cause us to perish;
For each wave is so clear,
Where the sea is deeper,
That we can see right down to the sea-bed,
And a great host of fish.[64]
We can see big and cruel fish -
We never heard talk of their like.
If the noise arouses them,
Be sure that we must die.'
The abbot smiled, and reprimanded them,
And judged them to be very foolish:
'Gentlemen, why are you afraid of anything?
How you thrust aside your beliefs!
You have suffered greater perils,
And God was a good guardian against them all.
This peril has not yet befallen you.
Confess your sins,'[65] Brendan said to them.
He sang more loudly and more resonantly.
Powerful beasts rise from the sea,

---

[64] Cf. Stokes, 'Máel Dúin (Suite),' pp. 54–57.
[65] Literally: 'Cry *Mea culpa*'

Vunt costeant la nef enturn,
Goïsant la feste del jurn.
Puis q'unt chantét que al jurn partint, 1065
Chescun peissun sa veie tint.

Avant curent, e veient cler
En mer halte un grant piler;
De naturel fud jargunce,
D'altre mairein n'i out unce; 1070
De jargunce fud saphire;
Riches estreit ki'n fust sire.
Desqu'as nües muntout ensus,
As funs de mer descendeit jus.
Uns paveiluns enturn i tent; 1075
Des le sumét en mer descent,
De or precius uvrét sutil–
Pur tut le mund faiz ne fust il.
Siglet Brandan icele part;
Ainz qu'i venget semblet lui tart. 1080
Sigle levét entret en tref
Od ses muines e od sa nef.
De smaragde veit un alter
U li pilers descent en mer;
Li sacraires fud sardoine, 1085
Li pavemenz calcedoine.

They go alongside the ship and all around it,
Enjoying the day's festival.
After the monks have sung that which was appropriate for
    the day,
Each fish continued along its way.

The Great Pillar and Canopy[66]

They pursue their course forward and see clearly
A great pillar in the open sea;
It was made of natural jacinth,
There was not an ounce of other material;
The jacinth was sapphire-blue;
Rich would be the possessor of it.
It ascended upwards as far as the clouds,
It went down as far as the bottom of the sea.
A canopy hangs around it;
From the top down into the sea it descends,
Delicately worked in precious gold –
It could not be made in exchange for all the world.
Brendan sails in that direction;
It seemed to him a long while before he arrived there.
With sail raised he enters into the canopy
With his monks and with his ship.
He sees an altar made of emerald
Where the pillars descend into the sea;
The shrine was made of sardonyx,
The pavement [of] chalcedony.

---

[66] Cf. Stokes, 'Máel Dúin (Suite),' pp. 52–55; Stokes, 'Húi Corra,' pp. 44–45.

Enz en piler fermét aveit
Tref de fin or: ço susteneit;
E les lampes sunt de beril.
Cil ne crement ci nul peril: 1090
Ici estunt desque al terz jurn.
Messes chantent tuit al lur turn.
Brandans en prent purpens en sei,
Ne deit querre le Deu secrei.
Dist as muines: Creés mun sen: 1095
Toluns d'ici, alum nus en.'
Un chalice mult festival
Prent li abes, tut de cristal;
Bient set, de Deu ne resortet,
Pur servir l'en quant l'en portet. 1100
Grant curs unt fait le pelerin,
Mais uncore ne sevent fin;
E nepurtant ne s'en feignent,
Mais cum plus vunt, plus se peinent,
Ne de peiner ne recrerrunt 1105
De ci que lur desir verrunt.

Apparut lur terre truble,
De neir calin e d'enuble;
De flaistre fum ert fumante,
De caruine plus puante; 1110
De grant nerçun ert enclose.
Cist ne rovent estre am pose,
E de mult luign unt or oït
Que la ne erent guaires goït.

Fixed into the pillar [of jacinth] there was
A beam of fine gold which supported [the altar];
And the lamps are made of beryl.
[The monks] fear no danger here;
They stay here until the third day.
They sing masses each in their turn.
Brendan makes up his mind,
He must not seek to understand God's mysteries.
He says to the monks: 'Trust my judgement:
Let us depart from here, let's go away.'
A very magnificent chalice
The abbot takes, all made of crystal;
He knows well that he is not being unfaithful to God,
Since he is taking it in order to do Him service therewith.
The pilgrims have covered a great distance,
But still they do not know the end;
And nevertheless they are not idle,
But the further they go the more they exert themselves,
They will not give up exerting themselves
Until they see what they desire.

The Smithy of Hell

An indistinct land appeared before them,
Of black fog and cloud;
It was smoking with putrid fumes,
Stinking more than rotting flesh;
It was surrounded by a great blackness.
[The monks] do not desire to take rest,
And from far away have now heard
That there they would hardly be welcome.

Mult s'esforcent de ailurs tendre, 1115
Mais ça estout lur curs prendre,
Quar li venz le les em meinet;
E li abes bein les enseignet,
E dit lur ad: 'Seignurs, sachez
Que a enfern estes cachez. 1120
N'oustes mester un mais si grant
Cum or avez de Deu guarant.'
Brandans ad fait sur eals la cruz:
Bein set, pres est d'enfern li puz.
Cum plus pres sunt, plus veient mal, 1125
Plus tenebrus trovent le val.
Des parfunz vals e des fosses
Lammes ardanz volent grosses;
De fous sufflanz li venz enruit,
Nuls tuneires si halt ne muit. 1130
Estenceles od les lammes,
Roches ardanz e les flammes
Par cel aïr tant halt volent
Le cler del jurn que lur tolent.

    Cun alouent endreit un munt, 1135
Virent un fed dunt poür unt;
Forment fud granz icil malfez,
D'enfern eisit tuz eschalfez;
Un mail de fer en puin portout–
A un piler asez i out. 1140
Cum s'aparçout par sun reguard
A uilz flammanz cun fus chi art,
E veit iceals, a tart li est
Que sun turment tut i ait prest.

The Anglo-Norman Voyage of St Brendan

They make great efforts to direct their course elsewhere;
But they must take their course that way,
For the wind led them there;
And the abbot explained to them clearly,
And has said to them: 'Gentlemen, be aware
That you are being driven towards Hell.
You never had greater need
Than you have now of God's protection.'
Brendan has made the sign of the cross on them:
He is well aware that the abyss of Hell is very near.
The nearer they get, the more evil they see,
The more they find the valley gloomy.
From the deep valleys and the pits
Big burning blades of metal fly;
The wind roars from blowing bellows,
No thunder makes such a noise.
Sparks with the burning blades,
Burning rocks and the flames
Fly so high on account of this violence
That they take away the light of day.
While they were going close by a mountain,
They saw a demon of whom they are afraid;
This demon was extremely big,
He came out of Hell well heated up;
He carried an iron hammer in his fist –
There was enough for a pillar.
As he became aware [of their presence][67]
He has flaming eyes like fires which burn,
And he sees [the monks], he longs
To prepare his instruments of torture.

---

[67] Literally: 'though his look'

Jetant flammes de sa gorge, 1145
A granz salz curt en sa forge.
Revint mult tost od sa lamme
Tute ruge cume flamme;
Es tenailes dun la teneit
Fais a dis bofs bien i aveit 1150
Halcet la sus vers la nue,
E dreit vers eals puis la rue;
Esturbeiluns plus tost ne vait,
Quant sus en l'air li venz le trait,
Ne li quarels d'arbaleste, 1155
Ne de funde la galeste.
Cum plus halcet, e plus enprent,
E en alant forces reprent;
Primes depart, puis amasset.
Ne cheot sur eals, ainz les passet. 1160
U cheit en mer, iloeches art
Cum brüere en un asart;
E mult lunc tens art la lame
Enz en la mer a grant flamme.
 Li venz la nef ad cunduite, 1165
Pur quei d'iloec pregnent fuite.
Al vent portant s'en alerent,
Mais la suvent reguarderent;
L'isle virent alumee
E cuverte de fumee. 1170

The Anglo-Norman Voyage of St Brendan

Spewing flames from his throat,
With great leaps he runs into the forge.[68]
He came back very quickly with his blade of metal
All red like a flame;
In the tongs with which he was holding it
There was a load which was quite enough for ten oxen.
He raises it up towards the cloud,
And then he hurls it straight towards them;
A whirlwind does not go more quickly,
When the wind draws it up into the air,
Nor does the bolt of a cross-bow,
Nor a missile hurled from a sling.
The higher it rises, the more it blazes,
And it gathers strength as it proceeds;
It first splits up, then combines again into one mass.
It does not fall on them, instead it passes beyond them.
Where it falls in the sea, there it burns
Like heather in a clearing;
And the blade burns for a very long time
With a big flame in the sea.
The wind has driven the ship onwards,
On account of which they flee from there.
They went away on the favourable wind,
But they often looked behind them;
They saw the island alight
And covered in smoke.

---

[68] Cf. Stokes, 'Máel Dúin (Suite),' pp. 53–55; Stokes, 'Húi Corra,' pp. 40–41 and 46–47.

Malsfeiz veient millers plusurs,
Criz de dampnez oënt e plurs.
Puur lur vent, mult forment grant,
Del fum chi luign par l'air se spant.
Endurent cum melz pourent, 1175
Eschiverent cum plus sourent.
Sainz hoem cum ad plusurs travailz–
De faim, de seif, de freiz, de calz,
Ainxe, tristur e granz poürs–
De tant vers Deu creist sis oürs. 1180
Eisi est d'els, puis q'unt voüd
U li dampnét sunt reçoüd.
En Deu ferment lur fiance,
N'i aturnent mescreance.
Vunt s'en avant, ne dutent rien, 1185
Quar ço sevent que espleitent bien.

Ne demurat fors al matin,
Virent un lu pres lur veisin:
Un munt cuvert de nublece;
Las meinet vent par destrecce. 1190
Vindrent i tost al rivage,
Mais mult ert de halt estage;
Nuls d'els trestuz choisir ne pout
La haltece que li munz out;
Vers la rive plus ne descent 1195

The Anglo-Norman Voyage of St Brendan

They see several thousand demons
They hear cries of the damned and weeping.[69]
The stench comes to them, exceedingly great,
From the smoke which spreads far through the air.
They put up with it as best they could,
They avoided [it] as much as they were able.
A holy man, when he has many hardships –
Of hunger, thirst, cold, heat,
Anxiety, sadness and great fears –
Increases proportionately his trust in God.[70]
So it is with them, after they have seen
Where the damned are lodged.
They make fast their trust in God,
And they are not inclined to lose faith.
They make their way forward, they fear nothing,
For they know that they are getting on well.

The Smoke-capped Mountain

As early as the next morning,
They saw a place close to them:
A mountain covered with clouds;
The wind took them there by force.
They soon came to the shore,
But it was of a very high elevation;
Not one of all of them could see
How high the mountain was;
Towards the shore it does not descend any more

---

[69] Cf. Stokes, 'Máel Dúin,' pp. 484–87.
[70] Burgess, 'La Souffrance et le repos,' pp. 267–77.

Que la u plus amunt s'estent;
E la terre est tute neire–
Tele nen out en tut l'eire.
Pur quel chose il ne sourent
Salt en l'uns fors; puis nel ourent. 1200
Tuit unt oïd qu'il lur ad dit,
Mais sul abes des uilz le vit:
'Seignur, de vus or sui preiez,
Pur mes pecchez, bien le creez.'
E li abes le veit traire 1205
A cent malfez chil funt braire.
Turnent d'iloec, ailurs en vunt;
Reguardent sei, quar poür unt.
Del fum li munz est descuvert,
Enfern veient tut aüvert. 1210
Enfers jetet fu e flammes,
Perches ardanz e les lammes,
Peiz e sufre desque as nües,
Puis sis receit, quar sunt sües.

Puis les meinet Brandans par mer, 1215
Des signacles les fait armer.
Veient en mer une boche,
Si cum ço fust une roche;
E roche fut verablement,
Mais nel qüient creablement. 1220
Dunc dist l'abes: 'Ne demurum;
Sachum que seit, si i curum.'
Vindrent ila, si truverent

The Anglo-Norman Voyage of St Brendan

Than there where it extends upwards
And the earth is completely black –
The like of which there had not been in their entire journey.
For what reason they did not know
One of them jumps out; then they didn't recover him.
They have all heard what he has said to them,
But only the abbot saw it with his eyes:
'My lord, I am now snatched away from you,
On account of my sins, believe it truly.'
And the abbot sees him dragged
By a hundred demons who make him howl.
They depart from there, they go elsewhere;
They look around, for they are afraid.
The mountain is no longer covered in smoke,
They see Hell quite open.
Hell discharges fire and flames,
Burning poles and blades of metal,
Pitch and sulphur right up to the clouds,
And then sucks them back in again, for they belong there.

Judas Iscariot

Then Brendan leads them across the sea,
Arming them with the sign of the cross.
They see a lump in the sea,
As if it were a rock;
And indeed, it was a rock,
But they do not credit it with any certainty.
Then the abbot says: 'Let us not tarry;
Let us find what it is and hurry towards it.'
And so they went there and they found

Içco que poi espeirerent:
Sur la roche u sunt venud 1225
Trovent seant un homme nud.
Mult ert pelfiz e detirez,
Delacherez e descirez;
D'un drap lïed sun vis aveit,
A un piler si se teneit. 1230
Fort se teneit a la pere,
Que nel rusast l'unde arere;
Undes de mer ferent le fort,
Pur quei n'ad fin la süe mort.
L'une le fert, pur poi ne funt; 1235
L'altre detriers jetet l'amunt;
Peril devant, peril desus,
Peril detriers, peril dejus;
Turmente grant ad a destre,
Nel ad menur a senestre. 1240
Quant l'unde ad fait les empeintes,
Mult lassement fait ses pleintes:
'Hai! pius Jesu, si jo osase,
Mercit de mei! jo criasse.
Hai! Jesu, reis de majestét, 1245
Faldrat ma morz n'ivern ne estét?
Jesu, chi moz tut le trone,
Ja est ta mercit itant bone;
Jesu, tant es misericors;
Ert nul' hure que seie fors? 1250
Jesu, li nez de Marie,
Ne sai si jo mercit crie.

The Anglo-Norman Voyage of St Brendan

That which they had little expected:
On the rock to which they had come
They found sitting a naked man.[71]
He was greatly plucked bare and battered,
Lacerated and torn;
His face was bound by a cloth,
He clung to a pillar.
Firmly he clung to the stone,
So that the waves would not drag him under;
The waves of the sea struck him strongly,
So that his death knew no end.
One struck him, to the point that he nearly perished;
The other, behind him, threw him upwards;
Danger in front; danger above,
Danger behind, danger below;
Great torment on the right
And no less on the left.
When the waves attacked,
With great weariness he made his laments:
'Oh! Holy Jesus, if I might be so bold,
Have mercy on me! I would cry.
Oh! Jesus, King of majesty,
Will my death not come about in winter nor summer?
Jesus, who moves the entire firmament,
Your mercy is already so good;
Jesus, you are so merciful;
Is there no time that I might be free?
Jesus, born of Mary,
I do not know whether I ought to cry for mercy.

---

[71] For a lexical discussion of Judas's suffering see Burgess, 'La Souffrance et le repos,' p. 275; also J.S. Mackley, 'The Torturer's "Art" in the Judas episode of Benedeit's *Voyage of St Brendan.*' *Notes and Queries* 54.1 (2007), pp. 24-27.

Ne puis, ne n'os, quar tant forfis
Que jugemenz de mei est pris.'
Quant le oit Brandans issi plaindre, 1255
Unches dolur nen out graindre;
Levet sa main, tuz les seignet,
D'apresmer la mult se peinet.
Cum apresmout, la mer ne mot,
Ne venz ne orrez ne la commot. 1260
Dist lui Brandans: 'Di mei, dolenz,
Pur quai suffres icez turmenz.
De part Jesu, qui tu crïes,
Jo te cumant quel mei dïes;
E certement me di qui es, 1265
E le forfait pur quei ci es.'
Pur le plurer Brandans ne pout
Avant parler, mais dunc se tout.
Cil respundit a voiz basse—
Mult ert roie, forment lasse: 1270
'Jo sui Judas, qui serveie
Jesu, que jo traïseie.
Jo sui qui mun seignur vendi,
E pur le doul si me pendi;
Semblant d'amur fis pur baiser, 1275
Descordai quant dui apaiser.
Jo sui qui sun aveir guardai,
En larrecin le debardai;
E l'offrande que hom li portout—
Tut' as povres il l'enhortout— 1280
Jo celoue en mes burses:
Pur oc me sunt peines surses;

The Anglo-Norman Voyage of St Brendan

I cannot, nor dare not, for I did so much wrong
That judgement has already been passed on me.'
When Brendan heard him lamenting so,
Never had he felt greater sorrow;
He raised his hand and made the sign of the cross over them all,
[And] made a great effort to approach.
As he approached the sea did not move,
No wind nor storm disturbed them.
Brendan said to him: 'Tell me, wretched man,
Why do you suffer this torment.
In the name of Jesus, to whom you cry,
I command you to tell me;
And to tell me truly who you are,
And what sin it is for.'
Brendan could speak no further for weeping)
So he became quiet.)
The other responded in a low voice –
It was very hoarse and very weary:
'I am Judas, who served
Jesus, whom I betrayed.
I am the man who sold my Saviour,
And for that sorrow I hanged myself;
Pretending love by giving a kiss,
And caused discord when I should have created peace.
I am he who kept his money,
And squandered it surreptitiously;
And the offerings that people brought to him –
[Which] he said should [be given] to the poor –
I concealed in my purse:
For this have sorrows befallen me;

E quidoue que fust celét
A lui qui fist cel estelét.
As povres Deu bein defendi; 1285
Or sunt riche, e jo mendi.
Jo sui li fels qui Deu haï
Le simple agnel as lus trahi.
Quant vi que as mains ert Pilate,
Dunc oi chere forment mate. 1290
Quant vi que as mains ert as Judus,
A ceals crüels liverez li pius,
Quant vi que as gabs l'aürouent,
E de spines coronouent,
Quant vi vilment que fud traitez, 1295
Sachez que fui mult dehaitez.
Puis vi que fud menez tüer,
Le dulz costed vi sanc süer.
Quant vi qu'en cruz esteit penduz,
E fud a mort de mei venduz, 1300
Les deners tost offri trente;
Cil ne voldrent cuilir rente.
Repentance nen oi sage,
Ainz me tuai par ma rage;
E quant confés ne me rendi 1305
Dampnez en sui de di en di.
Tu ne veiz rein de ma peine
Que enz en enfern jo demaine;
Cist est repos de mun peril,
Que al samadi prenc al seril. 1310
Dïemaine trestut le jurn

The Anglo-Norman Voyage of St Brendan

And I thought that it could be concealed
From him who made the starry heavens.
I denied succour to God's poor;
Yet, they are rich and I [am] a beggar.
I am the traitor who hated God,
[Who] handed the innocent lamb to the wolves.
When I saw that he was in the hands of Pilate,
Then I became very downcast.
When I saw he was in the hands of the Jews,
The holy man handed over to those cruel men,
When I saw that they "worshipped" him with derision,
And crowned him with thorns,
When I saw how badly he was treated,
Know that I was overcome by grief.
Then I saw that he was led to die,
I saw blood flow from his tender side.
When I saw him suspended on a cross,
And he was sold to death by me,
I quickly offered back the thirty pence;
But they were unwilling to accept repayment.
I did not repent prudently
Instead I killed myself in my madness;
And as I did not make my confession,
I am damned for all eternity.
You see nothing of the torment
That I undergo in Hell;
This is a respite from my danger,
That I receive on Saturday evening.
On Sunday, all day

Desque al vespre ai tel sujurn,
E del Noël la quinzeine
Ici deport ma grant peine,
E as festes la Marie 1315
Mes granz peines n'ai dunc mie;
Pasches e a Pentecoste
Fors tant cum veiz n'ai plus custe;
A feste altre en trestut l'an
N'ai entrebat de mun ahan. 1320
Dïemaine al aserir
D'ici m'en voi pur asperir.'
    Dunc dist Brandans: 'Ore me di,
Itel repos quant as ici,
En quels endreiz te demeines 1325
Es turmentes e es peines?
E es peines quel liu as tu?
D'ici quant moz, u en vas tu?'
Respunt Judas: 'Pres est li lius
As diables u est li fius; 1330
N'i ad guaires fors sul un poi:
Tant en sui luign que ci nes oi.
Dous enfers ad ci dejuste;
De suffrir les est grant custe.
Mult pres d'ici sunt dui enfern 1335
Qui ne cessent esteit ne ivern.
Li plus legiers est horribles,
A ceals qu'i sunt mult penibles;
Ço quident cil qui la peinent
Que altre vers eals mal ne meinent. 1340
For mei ne set uns suls de nus
Li quels des dous seit plus penus;

The Anglo-Norman Voyage of St Brendan

Until the evening I have such respite,
And for the fifteen days of Christmas
Here I am relieved of my great pain,
And on the feast of Mary
I have my great torment in no way then;
[At] Easter and at Pentecost
I have no more trouble than you see;
On other feasts in the course of the year
I have no respite from my distress.
On Sunday, when evening comes
I depart from here to suffer ill-treatment.'
Then Brendan said: 'Now tell me,
Since you have such respite here,
In what place do you dwell
[To endure] these torments and this suffering?
And in what place do you have these punishments?
When you move from here, where do you go?'
Judas replied: 'The place is near
To the devils where there is fire;
It is not far, only a short distance;
Far enough away that I do not hear them here.
There are two Hells close by here:
It is great trouble to suffer in them.
Very near here are two Hells
Whose [activity] never ceases summer or winter.
The lighter of the two is horrible,
And most painful to those who are there;
Those who suffer punishment there think
The others suffer no adversity in comparison.
Outside myself, not a single one of us knows
Which of the two is more painful;

N'est nuls plus ait que l'un des dous,
Mais jo chaitis ai amedous.
L'uns est en munt e l'autre en val, 1345
E sis depart la mer de sal;
Les dous enfers, mer les depart,
Mais merveille est que tute n'art.
Cil del munt est plus penibles,
E cil del val plus horribles; 1350
Cil pres del air calz e sullenz,
Cil pres de mer freiz e pullenz.
Ovoec la nuit un jurn sui sus,
Puis altretant demoir enjus;
Al un jurn munt, l'altre descent, 1355
N'est altre fin de mun turment;
Ne change enfern pur aleger,
Mais pur les mals plus agreger.
    Par le lundi e nuit e jurn
En la roe sui en tresturn, 1360
E jo chaitis, encroëz enz,
Turni tant tost cum fait li venz;
Venz la cunduit par tut cel air,
Todis m'en voi, todis repair.
Puis el marsdi en sui galiz, 1365
Cum cil qui est tot acaliz;
Ultre la mer vol enz en val
Al altre enfern u tant ad mal.
Iloces sui tost ferlïez,
De diables mult escrïez; 1370
El lit sui mis sur les broches,
Sur mei mettent plums e roches;

The Anglo-Norman Voyage of St Brendan

No one else has [to undergo] more than one of the two,
But I have endured misery in both.
One is on the mountain, the other is in the valley,
And the salty sea separates them;
The two Hells, separated by the sea,
But it is a marvel that [the sea] does not all burn.
That of the mountain is more painful[72]
And that of the valley is more horrible;
That near the sky is hot and sweaty,
That near the sea is cold and stinking.
For one night and one day I am there,
Then for just as long I remain below;
One day I rise, another I descend,
There is no end to my torment;
I do not change Hells to lighten [it]
But to make my suffering worse.

    On Monday, both night and day
I revolve on the wheel,
And wretch that I am, suspended there,
I whirl about as quickly as the wind does;
The wind drives it through the air,
Always I go round, always return.
Then on Tuesday I am hurled,
Like someone who is completely numb;
I fly over the sea into the valley
To the other Hell where there is so much suffering.
There I am soon chained,
Much reviled by devils;
I am laid on a bed of spits,
Upon me they place lead weights and rocks;

---

[72] Burgess: 'grievous'

Iloces sui se espeez
Que tant percét mun cors veez.
Al mercredi sus sui rüez, 1375
U li perilz mei est müez:
Pose del jurn buil en la peiz,
U sui si teinz cum ore veiz;
Puis sui ostét e mis en rost,
Entre dous fus lïed al post. 1380
Li post de fer fichet i est;
Se pur mei nun, pur el n'i est;
Tant est ruges cum si dis ans
En fu goüst as fols sufflanz;
E pur la peiz li fus s'i prent 1385
Pur enforcer le men turnment;
E dunc resui en peiz rüez,
Pur plus ardeir sui enlüez.
Nen est marbres nuls itant durs
Ne fust remis, se fust mis surs; 1390
Mais jo sui fait a cest' ire,
Que mis cors ne poit defire.
Itel peine, que que m'anuit,
Ai tut un jurn e une nuit.
Puis al jusdi sui mis en val, 1395
E pur suffrir contrarie mal
Dunches sui mis en un freid leu,
Mult tenebrus e forment ceu;
Tant i ai freid que mei est tart
Qu'el fu seie qui si fort art; 1400
E dunc m'est vis n'est turmente
Que del freid dunt plus me sente;
E de chescun si m'est avis
Ne seit si fort quant enz sui mis.

The Anglo-Norman Voyage of St Brendan

There I am so speared
That, [as] you see, my body is so full of holes.
On Wednesday I am hurled up,
Where my plight is changed:
For part of the day I am boiled in pitch,
When I am so stained, as you now [can] see;
Then I am removed and roasted,
Bound to a post between two fires.
The post of iron is fixed there;
It is there only for me, it is not there for the [others];
It is as red, as if for ten years
It has lain in a fire as bellows blow;
And because of the pitch, the fires take hold
To increase my torment;
And then I am hurled again into pitch,
I am smeared in order to burn more.
There is no marble so hard
That it would not be melted if it was placed on it;
Yet I am so inured to this torment,
That my body cannot perish.
And such torment, however it troubles me,
I have for a day and a night.
Then on Thursday I am put in the valley,
And to suffer the opposite torment
Accordingly I am placed in a cold place,
Very dark and extremely gloomy;
I am so cold that I long
To be in the fires that burn strongly;
And then it seems to me that there is no torment
That I could feel more than the cold;
And so each one does not seem to me
To be as strong when I am [first] placed in it.

Al vendresdi revenc amunt, 1405
U tantes morz cuntre mei sunt.
Dunc me scorcent trestut le cors,
Que de la pel n'at puint defors;
En la suie ovoec le sel
Puis me fulent od l'ardant pel; 1410
Puis me revant hastivement
Tuz nuvels quirs a cel turment.
Dis feiz le jurn bien me scorcent,
El sel entre puis m'esforcent;
E puis me funt tut cald beivre 1415
Le plum remis od le queivre.
Al samedi jus me rüent,
U li altre mals me müent;
E puis sui mis en gaiole–
En tut enfern n'at si fole, 1420
En tut enfer n'at si orde–
En li descen, e sanz corde.
Iloeces gis – n'i ai luur –
En tenebres e en puur.
Puurs i vent itant grande 1425
Ne guart quant mes quers espande;
Ne puis vomir pur le queivre
Que cil la me firent beivre;
Puis enfle fort, e li quirs tent;
Anguisus sui, pur poi ne fent. 1430
Tels calz, tels freiz e tels ulurs
Suffret Judas, e tels dolurs.
Si cum fud er al samedi
Vinc ci entre nune e midi;

The Anglo-Norman Voyage of St Brendan

On Friday I return upwards,
Where so many deaths await me.
Then they flay all my body,
So that nothing remains of my skin;
Then into soot [mixed] with salt)
They push me down with a burning stake;)
Then a completely new skin is formed)
As a result of this torment.)
Ten times a day they flay me,
Then they force me into the salt;
And then they make me drink scalding hot
The molten lead with copper.
On Saturday I am hurled down,
Where the other demons change my torment;
And then I am placed in a dungeon –
In all Hell there is nowhere so terrible,
In all Hell there is nowhere so filthy –
I go down there, and without a rope.
There I lie, I have no light –
In the darkness and the stench.
The stench comes there so greatly
That I am in constant fear that my heart will explode;
I cannot vomit on account of the copper
That the others made me drink in the other place;
I swell up greatly, my skin stretches;
I am full of anguish, I almost split.
Such heat, such cold and such stench
Judas suffers, and such sorrows.
Since yesterday was Saturday,
I came here in the early afternoon,[73]

---

[73] Literally, between nones and midday.

Hui mei repos a cest sedeir.	1435
Eneveies avrai mal seir:	
Mil deiables senés vendrunt;	
Ne avrai repos quant mei tendrunt.	
Mais si tu es de tel saveir,	
Anuit me fai repos aveir.	1440
Si tu es de tel merite,	
Anuit me fai estre quite.	
Bein sai que tu sainz es e puis,	
Quant sanz reguarz vens a tels lius.'	
Plurout Brandans a larges plurs	1445
D'iço que cist ad tanz dolurs;	
Comandet lui que lui dïet	
Que li dras deit dum se lïet	
E la pere u il se tint,	
Demandet dunt e de qui vint.	1450
Cil lui respunt: 'En ma vie	
Fis poi bien e mult folie.	
Li bien e mal or me perent	
Quel enz el quer plus chier m'erent.	
Del almoine que jo guardai	1455
A un nud fed drap acatai;	
Pur cel ai cest dun me lie	
Par la buche, que ne nie;	
Quant l'unde vent el vis devant,	
Alques par cest ai de guarant;	1460
Mais en enfern ne me valt rien,	
Quant de propre ne fud mun bien.	
A un' aigue fis un muncel,	
E puis desus un fort puncel,	

The Anglo-Norman Voyage of St Brendan

Today I have my rest sitting here.
Very soon I will have suffering in the evening:
One thousand devils will come forthwith;
I will have no respite when they get hold of me.
But if you have knowledge of such things,
Tonight make me have rest.
If you are of such merit,
Set me free tonight.
I know well that you are holy and pious,
Since you have come to such a place without fear.'
    Brendan cried great tears
Because this man had so many sorrows;
He told him to tell him
The meaning of the cloth with which he was bound,
And the stone to which he clung,
He asked where and from whom it came.
The other replied: 'In my life
I did little good and much evil.
I now understand the good and the evil
[And know] which in my heart were more dear to me.
From the alms which I kept
I bought a cloth for a naked wretch;
For this I am granted this gift which I wrap
Around my mouth so that I do not drown;
When the waves strike me full in my face,
I am somewhat protected by this;
But in Hell it is of no use to me,
For I did not buy it with my own money.
By a watercourse I made a hillock,
And then a strong little bridge over it,

U mult home periseient, 1465
Mais puis bien i guariseient;
Pur oec ai ci refrigerie
De si grande ma miserie.'
    Cum apresmount vers le primseir,
Dunc vit Brandans que cil dist veir: 1470
Veit i venir deiables mil
Od turmentes e grant peril;
E venent dreit a cel dolent;
Salt l'uns avant, al croc le prent.
Brandans lur dist: 'Laisez l'ici 1475
Desque al matin que seit lunsdi.'
Cil li dïent e calengent
Ne lairunt pas que nel prengent.
Dunc dist Brandans: 'Jol vus comant,
E de Jesu faz mun guarant.' 1480
Cil le laisent, e a force;
N'i unt nïent al estorce.
Brandans estait iloec la nuit;
N'i ad malfez qui mult n'annuit.
Deiables sunt del altre part; 1485
Ainz que seit jurz mult lur est tart;
A grant greine, a voiz truble,
Dïent que avrat peine duble.
Respunt l'abes: 'Ne avrat turment
Plus que ad oüd par jugement.' 1490
E puis qu'il fud cler ajurnét,
Od tut Judas s'en sunt turnét.
Brandans s'en vait d'iloec avant.

The Anglo-Norman Voyage of St Brendan

Where many men had perished,
But afterwards they passed unharmed;
For this I have this respite
From my so great misery.'
As nightfall approached,
Brendan saw that the man spoke the truth:
He sees a thousand devils coming
With torments and great danger;
And coming straight to this wretched man;
One leaps forward and seizes him with a crook.
Brendan says to them: 'Leave him here
Until Monday morning comes.'
They argue and dispute
They would not be prevented from taking him.
Then Brendan said: 'I command you,
And invoke Jesu as my protector.'
So they were compelled to leave him;
They have nothing in the end.
Brendan was there all night;
There was no devil that he wasn't very troublesome to.
Devils are around;
They are anxious for day to break;
With great grumbling, in raucous voices,
They say that he [Judas] will have twice the suffering.
The abbot replies: 'He will not have torment
More than he has been given by decree.'
And when it had become full daylight,
They departed with Judas.
Brendan goes on from there.

Bien set, de Deu ad bon guarant;
E li muine bien sevent tuit   1495
Que segur sunt el Deu cunduit.
Mercïent Deu de lur veies
E de tutes lur agreies.

Cum se numbrent li cumpaignun,
En lur cunte failent al un,   1500
E ne sevent qu'est devenuz,
Ne en quel leu est detenuz;
Des dous sevent cum unt errét,
Mais de cest terz sunt enserrét.
L'abes lur dist, qui tut le sout: 1505
'Deus en ad fait ço que li plout.
D'iço n'aiez nule dute,
Ainz tenez bien vostre rute.
Sachez qu'il ad sun jugement,
U de repos u de turment.'   1510

He knows well that he has God's protection;
And the monks all know
That they are safe with God's guidance.
They thank God for their voyage
And for all their equipment.[74]

A Monk Mysteriously Disappears[75]

When the companions count their number,
There is one missing in their count,
And they don't know what has become of him,
Nor in what place he has been detained;
They know how the first two have strayed,
But they are perplexed about the third.
The abbot, who knew everything, says to them:
'God has done with him what pleased Him.
Have no doubt about this,
Thus keep well on your course.
Be aware that judgement has been passed on him,
Either for rest or for torment.'

---

[74] 'agreies' – 'equipment', discussed in Waters, *Voyage*, p. 128; also T.D. Hemming, 'Language and Style in the *Voyage of Saint Brendan* by Benedeit,' *Littera et Sensus: Essays on Form and Meaning in Medieval French Presented to John Fox*, ed. D.A. Trotter (Exeter: University of Exeter Press, 1989), 1–16, p. 6.

[75] This scene has been added to the Anglo-Norman *Voyage* as Benedeit omits the scene concerning the Island of the Three Choirs in which the other supernumerary leaves the company in the *Nauigatio*.

Si cum il vunt, veient ester
Un munt mult halt tut sul en mer.
Tost i venent, mais la rive
Roiste lur est e escive.
L'abes lur dist: 'Istrai m'en fors.   1515
Ne movet uns fors sul mun cors.'
Puiet le munt e lunges vait
Ainz que trovét nul rien ait.
Par un rochét sa veie tint,
Une bodne puis i survint.   1520
Eisit uns hom tost de cel liu,
Religius semblout e piu.
Cil apelet Brandan avant–
Quar par Deu fud sun nun savant–
Puis le baiset; ses cumpaignuns   1525
Dist qu'amenget: ne failet uns.
Vait i Brandans, fait les venir,
Funt al rochét la nef tenir.
Cil les ad tuz numez par sei:
'Venez avant e baisez mei.'   1530
Cil li firent. Puis les menet
A sun estre, lur enseignet.
Cil reposent cum lur ad dit.
Merveillent lui e sun habit:
N'ad vestement fors de sun peil,   1535
Dum est cuvert si cum de veil;
Reguard aveit angelïel,

The Anglo-Norman Voyage of St Brendan

Paul the Hermit [76]

And as they travel, they see rising up
A very high mountain all alone in the sea.
They come quickly to it, but the shore
Is steep and difficult of access.
The abbot says to them: 'I shall disembark.
Let no one move except for myself.'
He ascends the mountain and goes for a long time
Before he has found anything.
His course took him through a rocky place,
Then a large smooth stone came into view.
A man came quickly from this place,
He seemed like a religious and pious man.
This man calls Brendan forward
For thanks to God, his name was known to him –
Then he kisses him; he tells him to bring his companions:
Let no one be missing.
Brendan goes [back] there, and gets them to come,
They make their ship fast to the rock.
This man has called each of them by his own name:
'Come forward and kiss me.'
This they did. Then he leads them
To his dwelling; he shows them [the way].
They rest as he has told them to.
They gaze with astonishment at him and his dress:
He has no clothing other than hair,
With which he is covered as if with a veil;
He had an angelic countenance,

---

[76] Cf. Stokes, 'Máel Dúin (Suite),' pp. 494–95.

E tut le cors celestïel;
N'est si blance neifs ne clere
Cume li peilz d'icest frere. 1540
　　Dist lui Brandans: 'Beal pere chers,
Di mei qui es.' Cil: 'Volunters.
Jo ai nun Pols li hermites.
De tuz dolurs sui ci quites.
Ci ai estét grant e lunc tens, 1545
E ça m'en vinc par Deu asens.
El secle fui hermite en bois:
Cele vie pris en mun cois.
Secund le sens, que aveie poi,
Deu serveie si cume soi; 1550
Il le cuilit par sa buntét,
Qu'a plus que n'est le m'at cuntét.
La me mandat, ci venisse
U ma glorie attendisse.
Cument i vinc? En nef entrai 1555
Tute preste cum la truvai;
Deus me cunduist tost e süef;
Quant arivai, ralat la nef.
Nunante anz ad qu'ai ci estét,
Beal tens i ad, tuzdis estét, 1560
Ici atent le juïse,
De Deu en ai cumandise;
Trestut i sui en carn e os,
Sanz mal que ai sui en repos.
Dunc a primes al jugement 1565
Le spirit del cors frat seivrement;
Od les justes resuscitrai

The Anglo-Norman Voyage of St Brendan

And his whole body celestial;
Snow is not so white or pure
As the hair of this brother.
Brendan says to him: 'Fair dear father,
Tell me who you are.' The other: 'Willingly.
My name is Paul the hermit.
I am free here from all pains.
I have been here for a very long time,
And I came away here under God's direction.
In my earlier life I was a hermit in the wood:
I chose this life.
In accordance with the little intelligence that I possessed,
I served God as well as I knew how to;
He accepted it in his kindness,
He has given me more credit for my service than I deserve.
He ordered me to come here
Where I should await my glory.[77]
How did I come here? I boarded a ship
Which I found quite ready;
God guided me quickly and calmly;
When I arrived, the ship went back.
I have been here for ninety years,
There is fine weather here, always summer;
Here I wait for the Last Judgement,
For that I have been commanded by God;
I am here in flesh and bone,
Without having any suffering I am at rest.
At the Last Judgement, then and no sooner,
The spirit will be separated from the body;
I shall rise again with the righteous

---

[77] Burgess: "Heavenly reward"

Pur la vie que segut ai.
Un sergant oi trent' anz pleiners,
De mei servir ert suveners: 1570
Uns lutres fud, qui m'aportout
Suvent peisun dun il me pout,
Tuzdis tres jurs la semaine;
Unckes nule ne fud vaine
Que treis peisuns ne me portast, 1575
Dun aveie mult pleiner past.
Al col pendud, marin werec
Plein un sacel portout tut sec,
Dun mes peisuns pouse quire.
Par qui ço fud, bien ert sire. 1580
Es primers anz que vinc ici
Tuz les trent' ans fui poüd si;
Des peisuns fud poüd si bien
Que n'oi mester de beivre rien;
N'ennuiout puint nostre Seignur 1585
De tel cunreid, ne de greignur.
Puis les trent' anz ne revint cil;
Nel fist surpeis, ne ne m'out vil,
Mais Deus ne volt que plus de fors
Venist cunreid pur sul mun cors. 1590
Ici me fist la funtaine,
De tuz cunreiz qui est pleine;
Ço li est vis, qui rien en beit,
De tuz cunreiz que saüls seit.
De aigue ai vescut anz seisante, 1595
Trent' a peisun, sunt nonante;
E el mund fui anz cinquante
Mis ethez est cent quarante.

The Anglo-Norman Voyage of St Brendan

On account of the life I have followed.
I had a servant for full thirty years,
He cared for me constantly:
He was an otter, who brought me
Often fish with which he fed me,
Three days every week;
Never was there any blank [week]
When he didn't bring me three fish,
So I had a copious supply of food.
Suspended around his neck)
He wore a small bag, full of completely dry seaweed,)
With which I could cook my fish.
It was a true Lord, through whom these things were done.
In the first years when I came here
For each of thirty years I was fed in this way;
I was fed so well on fish
That I did not need to drink anything;
Our Lord did not touble himself at all
To supply such provisions, nor anything else in addition
After the thirty years the otter did not come again;
It was not out of reluctance, nor did he [the otter] despise me,
But God no longer wished that from outside
Provisions came for my body alone.
Here He made me the spring,
Which is full of all food and drink;
It seems to him, who drinks anything from it,
That he is sated with all food and drink.
I have lived on water for sixty years,
Thirty on fish, that makes ninety;
And before that I was in the world fifty years:
My age is a hundred and forty.

Frere Brandan, or tei ai dit
Cument ici ai mun delit.   1600
Mais ti iras en paraïs;
Pres ad set anz que tu l'as quis.
Arere fras anceis return
Al bon hoste, u ous sujurn;
Il te menrat, e tu le siu,   1605
En paraïs u sunt li piu.
D'icest' aigue port'en od tei,
Dum guarisses de faim e sei.
Entre en ta nef, ne demurer;
Ne deit sun vent hom sururer.   1610
Dunet cungét, e cil le prent;
De ses beinfaiz graces l'en rent.

Or returnent vers lur hoste,
Si unt niule mult enposte.
Siglent lunges ainz qu'i veingent,   1615
Ja seit ço que dreit curs teingent,
E al jusdi de la ceine
La i venent a grant peine;
Iloec estunt cum soleient,
Desque de la muver deient.   1620
Le samadi al peisun vunt;
Cum altres anz la feste i funt,
E bien sevent qu'or ad set anz
Que li peisuns est lur servanz;
Deu en loënt, n'i unt perte,   1625
Par la vertud de Deu certe.

The Anglo-Norman Voyage of St Brendan

Brother Brendan, now I have told you
How I have my delight here.
But you will go to Paradise;
For almost seven years you have searched for it.
Before that you will return
To the good host, where you stayed;
He will lead you, and you follow him,
Into Paradise where the righteous are.
Take some of this water with you,
With which you should be protected from hunger and thirst.
Go back into your ship, do not be a long time;
A man must not overstay and miss a favourable wind.'
He gives his permission to depart, and Brendan takes his leave;
He gives thanks for his kindness.

The End of the Seventh Year

Now they turn back towards their host,
And the clouds are very dark.
They sail for a long time before they arrive,
Although they keep a straight course,
And on Maundy Thursday
They arrive there with great difficulty;
They stay there as is their wont,
Until they must move from there.
On Saturday they go to the fish;
As in the other years they celebrate the feast there
And they are well aware that now it is seven years
That the fish is their servant;
They praise God for this, they have not sustained any loss,
Because of God's most cerain power.

E l'endemain d'iloec movent
A itel vent cum il trovent;
Vers les oiseals tut dreit en vunt,
La u dous meis sujurnerunt;   1630
Iloec estunt a grant deduit,
E atendent le bon cunduit
Del bon hoste, qui frat od eals
L'eire qui est tant bons e beals.
Cil aprestet tuz lur busuinz,   1635
Quar bien saveit que l'eire est luinz;
E bien set tut que lur estot,
Pur ços guarnist de quanque poet.
Entrent en mer, l'ostes ovoec;
Ne revendrunt ja mais iloec   1640

Tendent lur curs vers orïent;
Del esguarer n'i funt nïent:
Tel i at enz en qui cunduit
Vunt a goie e a deduit.
A curs entrin, sanz defalte,   1645
Quarante dis en mer halte
Eisi curent que ne lur pert
Fors mer e cel qui sur eals ert;
E par l'otreid dei rei divin
Or aprisment vers le calin   1650
Qui tut aclot le paraïs
Dunt Adam fud poësteïs

And the following day they move from there
With such a wind as they find;
They go away straight towards the birds,
There where they will sojourn for two months;
There they stay in great happiness,
And await the favourable escort
Of their good host, who will make with them
The voyage which is so good and beautiful.
He prepared for all their needs,
For he was well aware that the journey is long;
And he is well aware of everything they need,
For these he provides whatsoever he can.
They put to sea, the host with them;
They will never return there again.

Paradise

They steer their course towards the east;
They do not lose their way at all:
As there is someone on board who is acting as escort
They proceed with joy and happiness.
With an unimpeded course, without interruption,
Forty days on the high seas
Thus they sail so that they see nothing
Apart from the sea and the heavens which were above them;
And with the permission of the divine king
Now they approached the fog
Which completely surrounded the Paradise
Over which Adam had dominion.

Nües grandes tenerge funt,
Que li sun eir return n'i unt.
Li granz calins tant aorbet,　　　　　　　1655
Qui i entret, tuz asorbet,
Si de Deu n'at la veüe
Qui poust passer cele nue.
Dunc dist l'ostes: 'Ne vus targez,
Mais le sigle de vent chargez.'　　　　　　1660
Cum aprisment, part la nue
Al espace d'une rue;
Cil se metent enz el calin,
E parmi unt un grant chemin.
Mult se fient en lur hoste　　　　　　　　1665
Pur la nue qu'unt encoste;
Grant est forment, e serree,
De ambes parz est amasse.
Treis jurz curent tut a plein curs
Par le chemin qui lur est surs;　　　　　　1670
El quart issent de cel calin;
Forment sunt led li pelerin.

 De la nue eisut s'en sunt,
E paraïs bien choisit unt.
Tut en primers uns murs lur pert,　　　　　1675
Desque as nües qui halcez ert;
N'i out chernel ne aleür
Ne bretesche ne nule tur.
Nuls d'els ne set en feid veire
Quel il seit faiz de materie,　　　　　　　1680
Mais blancs esteit sur tutes nefs:
Faitres en fut li suverains reis.

The Anglo-Norman Voyage of St Brendan

Great clouds make darkness,
Which ensures that [Adam's] heirs cannot return there.
The great fog blinds one so much,
That whoever enters it is completely blinded,
Unless God gives him the sight
Which could penetrate the cloud.
Accordingly the host said: 'Do not tarry,
But fill your sail with wind.'
As they approach, the cloud divides
To the width of a street;
[The monks] enter the fog,
And have a wide road through.
They put great trust in their host
On account of the cloud that they have alongside;
It is extremely big, and dense,
And it is heaped up on both sides.
For three days they sail all at full speed
Along the course which is before them;
On the fourth they come out of this fog;
The pilgrims are very glad.

    They have come out of the cloud,
And they have seen Paradise clearly.
First of all a wall appears to them,[78]
Which was built up right to the clouds;
There was neither battlement nor gallery
Nor parapet nor tower.
None of them knows with certainty
What material it might be made of,
But it was whiter than any snow:
The maker was the Sovereign King.

---

[78] Cf. Revelation 21:12–20.

Tuz ert entrins, sans antaile–
Unc al faire n'out travaile–
Mais les gemmes funt granz luurs,   1685
Dum purplantez esteit li murs.
As gutes d'or grisolites
Mult i aveit d'isselites;
Li murs flammet, tut abrase,
De topaze, grisopase,   1690
De jargunce, caldedoine,
De smaragde e sardoine;
Jaspes od les amestistes
Forment luisent par les listes;
Li jacinctes clers i est il   1695
Od le cristal e le beril;
L'un al altre dunet clartét
Chis asist fud mult enartét.
Luur grande s'entreportent
Des colurs chi si resortent.   1700
Li munt sunt halt, de marbre dur,
U la mer bat mult luign del mur;
E desure le mult marbrin
La muntaine est, tute d'or fin
E puis desus estait li murs,   1705
De paraïs qui clot les flurs.
Teles est li murs, si surplantez,
Qui doust estre de nus hantez.

    Tendent tut dreit vers la porte,
Mais l'entrée mult ert forte: 1710
Draguns i at qui la guardent;
Si cume fus trestut ardent.

The Anglo-Norman Voyage of St Brendan

Everything was in one piece, without incisions –
There was never any labour in making it –
But the gems shine very brightly,
With which the wall was studded.
There were many exquisite chrysolites)
Containing drops of gold;   )
The wall blazes, all is on fire,
With topaz, chrysoprase,
With jacinth, chalcedony,
With emerald and sardonyx;
Jasper along with amethysts
Shine brightly around the edges;
The jacinth there is bright
With crystal and beryl;
The one gives brightness to the other.
The person who set them was very skilled.
They convey great light to each other
From the colours which thus flash back.
The hills are high, of hard marble,
Where the sea beats upon the shore very far from the wall;
And above the marble hill
Stands [another] mountain, all of fine gold;
And then above the mountain stood the wall,
Which encloses the flowers of Paradise.
Such is the wall, set so on high,
Which ought to have been inhabited by us.
They head straight for the gate,
But it was very difficult to enter:
There are dragons guarding it;
And they are all burning like fire.

Dreit al entrer pent uns glavies–
Qui cel ne crient nen est savies–
La mure aval, le helt amunt; 1715
N'est merveille si poür unt.
En aines pent, e turnïet;
Sul del vedeir esturdïent;
Fer ne roche ne adamant
Ne pot guarir a sun trenchant. 1720
Puis unt veüd un juvencel
Qui veint cuntre eals, mult forment bel;
E cil se fait Deu message,
Dist que vengent a rivage.
Il arivent; cil les receit, 1725
Tuz le numet par lui nun dreit;
Puis dulcement les ad baisez,
E les draguns tuz apaisez:
Fait les gesir cuntre terre
Mult humblement e sanz guerre; 1730
E le glaive fait retenir
A un angele qu'il fair venir,
E l'entrée est uverte.
Tuit entrent en glorie certe.
    Avent en vait cil juvenceals, 1735
Par paraïs vait ovoec eals.
De beals bois e de rivere
Veient terre mult plenere;

The Anglo-Norman Voyage of St Brendan

Right at the entrance hangs a sword –
He who does not fear this is not wise –
The point downwards, the hilt upwards;
It is no wonder if they are afraid.
It hangs suspended, and whirls round;[79]
Just seeing it makes one dizzy;
Neither iron nor rock nor diamond
Can be undamaged by its sharp edge.
Then they have seen a young man[80]
Who comes towards them, very, very handsome;
And he is God's messenger,
He tells them to come ashore.
They land; [the youth] welcomes them,
He calls them all by their correct name;
Then he has kissed them gently,
And calmed all the dragons down:
He makes them lie on the ground
Quite humbly and without resistance;
And he causes the sword to be held back
By an angel whom he summons,
And the entrance is open.
They all enter in true glory.
This young man goes ahead,
He walks through Paradise with them.
They see a very fertile land;   )
Of fine woods and meadow-land)

---

[79] Genesis 3: 24; for a discussion of 'En aines pent', see John Orr, 'Old French *en aines*,' *Modern Language Review* 22 (1927): 199–201.
[80] In Burgess's translation the Host and the Youth are the same person.

Gardins est la praierie,
Qui tuzdis est beal flurie.   1740
Li flur süef mult i flairent,
Cum la u li piu repairent,
D'arbres, de flurs delicius,
De fruiz, d'udurs mult precius.
De runceie ne de cardunt   1745
Ne de orthie n'i ad fusun;
D'arbre n'erbe n'i ad mie
Ki süaté ne rechrie.
Flurs e arbres tuzdis chargent,
Ne pur saisun unc ne targent;   1750
Esteit süef tuzdis i est,
Li fruiz de arbres e de flurs prest,
Bois repleniz de veneisun,
E tut li flum de bon peisun.
Li flum i sunt qui curent lait.   1755
Cele plentét par tut en vait.
La ruseie süet le mel
Par le ruseit qui vient del cel.
Si munt i at, cil est tut d'or;
Si grant pere, i at tensor.   1760
Sanz fin i luist, li clers soleil,
Ne venz n'orez n'i mot un peil;
N'i vient nule nue del air
Qui del soleil tolget l'esclair.
Chi ci estrat, mal n'i avrat,   1765
Ne dunt mals vent ja nel savrat,
Ne chalz, ne freiz, ne dehaite,
Ne faim, ne seit, ne suffraite;

The Anglo-Norman Voyage of St Brendan

The meadow,)
Which is perpetually fair with flowers, is a garden)
The flowers smell very sweet there,
As [befits] where the pious dwell,
With trees and delightful flowers,
[And] superb fruits and scents.
Neither of brambles nor of thistles
Nor of nettles is there any abundance;
There is no tree nor herb at all
Which does not exude sweetness.
Flowers and trees always produce fruit,
Nor do they ever wait for any season;
It is always pleasant summer there
The fruit of trees and flowers [are] always ready,
The wood always filled with game,
And all the rivers with good fish.
The rivers there flow with milk.
This abundance is everywhere.
The reeds exude honey
On account of the dew which descends from heaven.
And there is a mountain all of gold;
And there is a big stone, it is treasure.[81]
The bright sun shines there without end,
Neither wind, nor breeze makes a hair move there;
No cloud comes into the air there
Which would take away the brightness of the sun.
He who will be here will have no suffering there,
Nor will he ever know whence evil comes,
Neither heat, nor cold, nor affliction,
Nor hunger, nor thirst, nor privation;

---

[81] Burgess: 'No treasure house has a stone so massive'.

De tuz ses bons avrat plentét.
Ço que plus est sa voluntét, 1770
Cel ne perdrat, suurs en est;
Tuzdis l'avrat e truvrat prest.
    Bien vait Brandans cele goie.
L'urel semblet forment poie
Qu'il i estait a ço vedeir 1775
Lunges voldrat ileoc sedeir.
Mult bien avant l'ad cil menét,
De multes riens l'ad asenét;
Bien diviset, e si li dit
De quel avrat chascuns delit. 1780
Vait cil avant, e cist aprés
Sur un halt munt cume ciprés;
D'ici veient avisuns
Dum ne sevent divisiuns.
Angeles veient, e sis oient 1785
Pur lur venir cum s'esgoient;
Oient lur grant melodie,
Mais nel poient suffrir mie:
Lur nature ne poet prendre
Si grant glorie, ne entendre. 1790
Cil lur ad dit: 'Returnum nus,
Avant d'ici ne menrai vus;
Ne vus leist pas aler avant,
Quar poi estes a ço savant.
Brandans, tu veis cest paraïs 1795
Que tu a Deu mult requeïs.
De la glorie cent mille tant
Que n'as veüd, ad ça avant.

The Anglo-Norman Voyage of St Brendan

He will have all his desires in abundance.
No matter how great is his desire
He will not lose that, he is sure of it;
He will have it every day and will find it ready.
    Brendan sees this joy clearly.
The space of time seemed to him extremely short
When he remained there to see this;
He wanted to sit there for a long time.
[The youth] has led him a long way forward,
And he has instructed him about many things;
He explains well in detail, and so tells him,
What delights awaited each of them.[82]
[The youth] goes in front, and [Brendan] after,
On to a high mountain like a cypress;
From here they see wonderful sights
For which they know no explanations.
They see angels, and hear
How they are rejoicing at their coming;
They hear their great melody,
But they cannot stand it at all:
Their nature cannot comprehend
Such great rejoicing, nor listen to it.
[The youth] has said to them: 'Let's go back,
I will not take you on further from here;
You are not permitted to go further,
For you possess too little knowledge for this.
Brendan, you see this Paradise
For which you have frequently besought God.
Farther on there is a hundred thousand times more glory)
Than you have seen.)

---

[82] Literally, 'About which delights each one will have.'

A ore plus n'i aprendras,
Devant iço que revendras.   1800
O or venis si carnalment
Tost revendras spiritualment.
Or t'en reva; si revendras,
Le juïse ci atendras.
De cez peres en fai porter   1805
A enseignes de conforter.'
Puis que out ço dit, il en alat,
A enseignes peres portat.

Brandans de Deu cungét ad pris
E as chers sainz de paraïs.
Li juvenceals les en cunduit,
Desqu'en la nef sunt entrét tuit,
Puis ad sur eals seignacle fait.
Mult tost unt sus lur sigle fait.
Ileoc remist lur hostes pius,   1815
Quar paraïs fud sis dreiz fius.
E cil s'en vunt haitïement,
Nen unt d'orez retenement;
En treis meis sunt en Irelande
Par la vertud de Deu grande.   1820
   Ja nuvele vait par païs
Que venuz est de paraïs.
Ne sunt haitét sul si parent,
Ainz sunt trestuz comunement.

Now you will not learn any more about it,
Before you return.
Where you now came in body
Soon you will return in spirit.
Now off you go; and you will come back,
You will await the Last Judgement here.
Take away these precious stones
As tokens of hope.'
Then when [the youth] had said this, [Brendan] went away,
He carried [the] stones as tokens.

Brendan's Return and Death

Brendan has taken his leave of God
And of the beloved holy men of Paradise.
The youth leads them away,
Until they have all boarded the ship,
Then he has made the sign of the cross on them.
Very soon they have hoisted their sail.
There their pious host remained,
For Paradise was his rightful estate.
And the monks sail away joyfully,
They have no hindrance from the breeze;
Within three months they are in Ireland
Thanks to God's great power.
Already the news is travelling through the land
That he has come from Paradise.
His kinsmen are not alone in rejoicing,
But everyone is universally joyful.

Sur tuz sunt leid si cher frere 1825
De ço qu'or unt lur dulz pere.
Suvent lur dit cum unt errét
U furent bien, u enserrét
E si lur dist cum prest truvat
Quanque busuign a Deu ruvat; 1830
En l'un e l'el, trestut lur dist,
Cum il truvat ço que il quist.
La plusur d'els ensaintirent
Par la vertud qu'en lui virent.
Tant cum Brandans el secle fud, 1835
A mulz valut par Deu vertud.
Quant vint al tens que il finat,
Ralat u Deus lui destinat.
El regne Deu, u alat il,
Par lui en vunt plusur que mil. 1840

Explicit Vita Sancti Brendani

The Anglo-Norman Voyage of St Brendan

In particular his dear brethren are glad
Because they have now got their kind father back.
He often told them how they have wandered,
Where they were content, and where they were in distress;
And he also told them how he found a ready response
When he asked God for anything he needed;
And one thing and another, he told them everything,
How he found that which he sought.
Several of them embarked on a saintly life
On account of the power that they saw in him.
As long as Brendan was in this earthly life,
He assisted many thanks to God's power.
When it came to the time that he died
He went back where God destined him.
Into the kingdom of God, where he went,
More than a thousand go because of him.

Here ends the life of St Brendan

Bibliography and further reading

Allen, J.B. and Daniel G. Calder. *Sources and Analogues of Old English Poetry: The Major Latin Texts in Translation*. Cambridge: D.S. Brewer Ltd., 1970.

Ashe, Geoffrey. *Land to the West*. London: Collins, 1962.

Barron, W.R.J. *English Medieval Romance*. London: Longman, 1987.

Benedeit. *The Anglo Norman* Voyage of St Brendan. Eds. Ian Short and Brian Merrilees. Manchester: Manchester University Press, 1979.

Béroul. *The Romance of Tristran*. Trans. Norris J. Lacy. New York and London: Garland Publishing Inc., 1989.

Biller, Peter, Caterina Bruschi and Shelagh Sneddon (eds.). *Inquisitors and Heretics in Thirteenth-Century Languedoc: Edition and Translation of Toulouse Inquisition Depositions, 1273-1282*. Leiden: Brill, 2010.

Borsje, Jacqueline. *From Chaos to Enemy: Encounters with Monsters in Early Irish Texts. An Investigation Related to the Process of Christianization and the Concept of Evil*. Instrumenta Patristica, 29. Steenbrugge: St-Pieters abdij; Turnhout: Brepols, 1996.

Brown, A.C.L. 'Barintus.' *Revue celtique* 22 (1901). 339–44.

Brown, A.C.L. *The Origins of the Grail Legend*. New York: Russell and Russell, 1966.

Burgess, Glyn S. 'Repetition and Ambivalence in the *Anglo-Norman Voyage of St Brendan*.' *Anglo-Norman Anniversary Studies*. Ed. Ian Short. London: Anglo-Norman Text Society, 1993. 61–74.

Burgess, Glyn S. '*Savoir* and *faire* in the Anglo-Norman *Voyage of St Brendan*.' *French Studies* 49 (1995). 257–74.

Burgess, Glyn S. 'Les fonctions des quatre éléments dans le *Voyage de saint Brendan* par Benedeit.' *Cahiers de Civilisation Médiévale X^e–XIIe siècles* 38 (1995). 3–22.

Burgess, Glyn S. 'La Souffrance et le repos dans *Le Voyage de saint Brendan* par Benedeit.' *Miscellanea Mediaevalia: Mélanges offerts à Philippe Ménard*. Vol. 1. Paris: Champion, 1998. 267–77.

The Anglo-Norman Voyage of St Brendan

Burgess, Glyn S. 'The Anglo-Norman Version' in *The Voyage of St Brendan: Representative Versions of the Legend in English Translation*. Eds. W.R.J. Barron and Glyn S. Burgess. Exeter: University of Exeter Press, 2002; 2nd Revised edition 2005. 65–102.

Burgess, Glyn S. 'The Use of Animals in Benedeit's Version of the Brendan Legend.' *The Brendan Legend: Texts and Versions*. Eds. Glyn S. Burgess and Clara Strijbosch. Leiden: Brill, 2006. 11–34.

Burgess, Glyn S., and Clara Strijbosch, eds. *The Brendan Legend: Texts and Versions*. Leiden: Brill, 2006.

Burgess, Glyn S., and Clara Strijbosch. *The Legend of St Brendan: A Critical Bibliography*. Dublin: Royal Irish Academy, 2000.

Byrne, Mary E. 'On the Punishment of Sending Adrift.' *Ériu* 11 (1932). 97–102.

Carney, James. '*Navigatio sancti Brendani abbatis* (Review).' *Medium Aevum* 22 (1963): 37–44; repr. in *The Otherworld Voyage in Early Irish Literature*. Ed. Jonathan M. Wooding. Dublin: Four Courts Press, 2000. 42–51.

Childress, Diana T. 'Between Romance and Legend: "Secular Hagiography" in Middle English Literature.' *Philological Quarterly* 57 (1978). 311–22.

de Paor, Liam ed. *Saint Patrick's World*. Dublin: Four Courts Press, 1993.

de Voragine, Jacobus. *Legenda Aurea*. Ed. Thomas Graesse. Osnabrück: Otto Zeller Verlag, 1969.

Delehaye, Hippolye. *The Legends of the Saints*. Trans. Donald Attwater. London: Geoffrey Chapman, 1962.

Dumville, David M. '*Echtrae* and *Immram*: Some Problems of Definition.' *Ériu* 27 (1976). 73–94.

Frye, Northrop. *Anatomy of Criticism*. Princeton and Oxford: Princeton University Press, 1971.

Gardiner, Eileen. *Visions of Heaven and Hell before Dante*. New York: Italica Press, 1989.

Heist, W.W. *Vitae sanctorum Hiberniae*. Brussels: Société des Bollandistes, 1965.

Hemming, T.D. 'Language and Style in the *Voyage of Saint Brendan* by Benedeit.' *Littera et Sensus: Essays on Form and Meaning in Medieval French Presented to John Fox*. Ed. D.A. Trotter. Exeter: University of Exeter Press, 1989). 1–16.

Herbert, Máire. 'Literary Sea-Voyages and Early Munster Hagiography' in *Celtic Connections: Proceedings of the 10th Congress of Celtic Studies*. Eds. Ronald Black, William Gillies and Roibeard Ó Maolalaigh, vol. 1: Language, Literature, History, Culture. East Linton: Tuckwell Press Ltd., 1999. 182–189.

Horstmann, Carl. *The Early South English Legendary or lives of saints: 1, MS Laud, 108, in the Bodleian Library*. EETS OS 87. London; N. Trübner & Co, 1887.

Hull, Eleanor. 'The Silver Bough in Irish Legend,' *Folklore* 12 (1901). 430–45.

Illingworth, R.N. 'The Structure of the Anglo-Norman *Voyage of St Brendan* by Benedeit.' *Medium Aevum* 55 (1986): 217–29.

Johnston, Elva. 'A Sailor on the Seas of Faith: The Individual and the Church in *The Voyage of Máel Dúin*.' *European Encounters: Essays in Memory of Albert Lovett*. Eds Judith Devlin and Howard B. Clarke. Dublin: University College Dublin Press, 2003. 239–52.

Jones, Robin F. 'The Mechanics of Meaning in the Anglo-Norman *Voyage of Saint Brendan*.' *Romanic Review* 71 (1980). 105–13.

Jones, Robin F. 'The Precocity of Anglo-Norman and the *Voyage of Saint Brendan*.' *The Nature of Medieval Narrative*. Eds Minnette Grunmann-Gaudet and Robin F. Jones. *French Forum Monographs* vol. 22. Lexington, Kentucky: French Forum Publishers, 1980.

Kaland, Sigrid. 'Comments on The Early Settlement of Iceland.' *Norwegian Archaeological Review* 24 (1991). 10–12.

Larmat, Jean. 'L'Eau dans la *Navigation de Saint Brandan* de Benedeit.' *L'Eau au Moyen Age*. Senefiance 15. Aix-en-Provence: CUER MA, 1985.

Lane, Edward William. *The Thousand and One Nights*. 3 vols. London: Charles Knight and Co., 1841.

Legge, M. Dominica. '*Letre* in Old French.' *Modern Language Review* 56 (1961). 333–34.

Legge, M Dominica. *Anglo-Norman Literature and its Background.* Oxford: Clarendon Press, 1963.

Lewis, C.S. *The Discarded Image.* Cambridge: Cambridge University Press, 1967.

Little, George A. *Brendan the Navigator.* Dublin, M.H. Gill and Son Ltd, 1945.

Mac Mathúna, Séamus 'Contributions to a Study of the Voyages of St Brendan and St Malo.' *The Otherworld Voyage in Early Irish Literature.* Ed. Jonathan M. Wooding. Dublin: Four Courts Press, 2000. 157–74.

Mac Mathúna, Séamus. *Immram Brain: Bran's Journey to the Land of the Women.* Tübingen: M. Niemeyer, 1985.

Mac Mathúna, Séamus. 'The *Irish Life of Saint Brendan*: Textual History, Structure and Date.' *The Brendan Legend: Texts and Versions.* Eds. Glyn S. Burgess and Clara Strijbosch. Leiden: Brill, 2006). 117–58.

Mackley, J.S. 'The Torturer's "Art" in the Judas episode of Benedeit's *Voyage of St Brendan*.' *Notes and Queries* 54 (2007). 24-27.

Mackley. J.S. *The Legend of St Brendan: A Comparative Study of the Latin and Anglo-Norman Versions.* Leiden: Brill, 2008.

Meyer, Kuno, ed. *The Voyage of Bran, Son of Febal, to the Land of the Living: an Old Irish Saga.* 2 vols. London: D. Nutt, 1895–1897.

Meyer, Paul. 'Satire en vers rythmiques sur la légende de saint Brendan.' *Romania* 31 (1902).

Moran, Patrick F. ed. *Acti Sancti Brendani: Original Latin Documents connected with the Life of Saint Brendan, Patron of Kerry and Clonfert.* Dublin: Kelly, 1872.

Muir, Bernard J. *The Exeter Anthology of Old English Poetry.* 2 vols. Exeter: University of Exeter Press, 1994.

O'Donoghue, Denis ed. *Lives and Legends of Saint Brendan the Voyager.* Felinfach: Llanerch, 1994.

O'Loughlin, Thomas. 'Distant Islands: The Topography of Holiness in the *Nauigatio sancti Brendani*.' *The Medieval Mystical Tradition in England, Ireland and Wales.* Ed. Marion Glasscoe. Cambridge: D.S. Brewer, 1999. 1-20.

Orchard, Andy. *Pride and Prodigies: Studies in the Monsters of the Beowulf-Manuscript*. Toronto: University of Toronto Press, 1995.

Orr, John 'Old French *en aines*.' *Modern Language Review* 22 (1927). 199–201.

Patch, Howard Rollin. *The Other World According to Descriptions in Medieval Literature*. Cambridge, Mass.: Harvard University Press, 1950.

Plummer, Charles. *Vitae sanctorum Hiberniae*. 2 vols. Oxford: Clarendon Press, 1910.

Plummer, Charles. *Lives of the Irish Saints*. 2 vols. Oxford, Clarendon Press, 1922.

Rumsey, Patricia M. *Sacred Time in Early Christian Ireland*. London: T & T Clark Ltd, Continuum, 2007.

Selmer, Carl ed. *Navigatio Sancti Brendani abbatis from Early Latin Manuscripts*. Publications in Mediaeval Studies, 16. Notre Dame: University of Notre Dame Press, 1959.

Severin, Timothy. *The Brendan Voyage*. London: Abacus, 1996.

Sharpe, Richard. *Medieval Irish Saints: An Introduction to the Vitae sanctorum Hiberniae*. Oxford: Clarendon Press, 1991.

Short, Ian. '*Tam Angli Quam Franci*: Self-definition in Anglo-Norman England.' *Anglo-Norman Studies* 18 (1995). 153–75.

Short, Ian and Merrilees, Brian. *Le Voyage de Saint Brendan, éd. bilingue, texte, traduction, présentation et notes*. Paris: Champion Classiques, 2006.

Sneddon, C.R. 'Brendan the Navigator: A Twelfth-Century View.' *The North Sea World in the Middle Ages*. Eds Thomas R. Liszka and Lorna E.M. Walker. Dublin: Four Courts Press, 2001. 211–29.

Stokes, Whitley. 'Notes on the Life of St Brendan.' *Irish Ecclesiastical Record* 8 (October 1871–February 1872). 17–25, 79–86, 178–190 and 193–208.

Stokes, Whitley. 'The Voyage of Snedgus and Mac Riagla.' *Revue celtique* 9 (1888). 14–25.

Stokes, Whitley. 'The Voyage of Máel Dúin.' *Revue celtique* 9 (1888). 447–95.

Stokes, Whitley. 'The Voyage of Máel Dúin (suite).' *Revue celtique* 10 (1889). 50–95.

Stokes, Whitley. 'The Voyage of the Húi Corra.' *Revue celtique* 14 (1893). 22–69.

Strickland, Agnes. *The Lives of the Queens of England*. London: Henry Colburn, 1840.

Strijbosch, Clara. 'Searching for a Versatile Saint' in *The Brendan Legend: Texts and Versions*. Ed. G.S. Burgess and Clara Strijbosch. Leiden: Brill, 2006.

Tierney, J.J., ed. *Dicuili Liber de mensura orbis terrae*. Dublin: Dublin Institute for Advanced Studies, 1967.

Thorgilsson, Ari. *Landnámabók*. Trans. Thomas Ellwood. Kendal: T. Wilson, 1898.

Wahlberg, E. 'Sur le nom de l'auteur du *Voyage de saint Brendan*.' *Studia Neophilologica* 12 (1939). 46-55.

Waters, E.G.R. ed. *The Anglo-Norman Voyage of St Brendan by Benedeit*. Oxford: Clarendon Press, 1928.

Weaver, J.R.H. ed. *The Chronicle of John of Worcester 1118–1140*. Oxford: Clarendon Press, 1908.

Wollin, Carsten. 'The *Navigatio sancti Brendani* and Two of its Twelfth-Century Palimpsests: The Brendan Poems by Benedeit and Walter of Châtillon'. *The Brendan Legend: Texts and Versions*. Eds. G.S. Burgess and Clara Strijbosch. Leiden: Brill, 2006. 281–313.

Wooding, Jonathan M. 'Introduction' in *The Voyage of St Brendan: Representative Versions of the Legend in English Translation*. Eds. W.R.J. Barron and Glyn S. Burgess. 2nd ed. Exeter: University of Exeter Press, 2005. 1–12.

Wooding, Jonathan M. (ed.). *The Otherworld Voyage in Early Irish Literature*. Dublin: Four Courts Press, 2000.

Wooding, Jonathan M. 'The Date of the *Nauigatio S. Brendani Abbatis*.' *Studia Hibernica*, vol. 37, 2011. 9–26.

ABOUT THE AUTHOR

J.S. Mackley is a Senior Lecturer in English and Creative Writing at the University of Northampton. He studied a degree in English Studies at the University of Stirling, and an MA and PhD in Late Medieval Studies and English, both at the University of York.

He is author of *The Legend of St Brendan: A Comparative Study of the Latin and Anglo-Norman Versions* and *The Origin of the Giants: The First Settlers of Albion: Bilingual Edition*. He has recently finished editing a Gothic novel last published in 1802 entitled *Who's the Murderer* by Eleanor Sleath (forthcoming from Valancourt Press). He is one of the editors of *Creating Myths as Narratives of Empowerment and Disempowerment* (forthcoming from University of Jendouba Press).

He has also written articles on St Brendan, gothic literature, fantasy literature and more recently, English mythology. He is currently working on a translation of a treatise on cosmography.

www.ingramcontent.com/pod-product-compliance
Lightning Source LLC
Chambersburg PA
CBHW071159070526
44584CB00019B/2848